D0775585

Extraordinary Time

Extraordinary Time

Spiritual Reflections
from a Season with Cancer, Death, and Transition

Laura Dunham

CASCADE *Books* • Eugene, Oregon

EXTRAORDINARY TIME
Spiritual Reflections from a Season with Cancer, Death, and Transition

Copyright © 2018 Laura Dunham. All rights reserved. Except for brief quotations in critical publications or reviews, no part of this book may be reproduced in any manner without prior written permission from the publisher. Write: Permissions, Wipf and Stock Publishers, 199 W. 8th Ave., Suite 3, Eugene, OR 97401.

Cascade Books
An Imprint of Wipf and Stock Publishers
199 W. 8th Ave., Suite 3
Eugene, OR 97401

www.wipfandstock.com

PAPERBACK ISBN: 978-1-5326-4594-5
HARDCOVER ISBN: 978-1-5326-4595-2
EBOOK ISBN: 978-1-5326-4596-9

Cataloguing-in-Publication data:

Names: Dunham, Laura, author.

Title: Extraordinary time : spiritual reflections from a season with cancer, death, and transition. / Laura Dunham.

Description: Eugene, OR: Cascade Books, 2018 | Includes bibliographical references.

Identifiers: ISBN 978-1-5326-4594-5 (paperback) | ISBN 978-1-5326-4595-2 (hardcover) | ISBN 978-1-5326-4596-9 (ebook)

Subjects: LCSH: Suffering. | Death. | Holiness.

Classification: BT767 .D80 2018 (print) | BT767 (ebook)

Manufactured in the U.S.A.   AUGUST 22, 2018

New Revised Standard Version Bible, copyright 1989, Division of Christian Education of the National Council of the Churches of Christ in the United States of America. Used by permission. All rights reserved.

For my Communion of Saints both here and there,
with love and gratitude for accompanying me through my
extraordinary time
and every day before and since.

Contents

Introduction

HAVE YOU EVER HEARD it said that God never gives us more than we can handle? You might want to think twice before telling that to someone in the midst of a crisis. When we are being sorely tested, we're looking for serious help, not a remark, however kindly meant, that adds insult to injury. Later, after we've survived and are able to get some perspective on what happened, we may be able to hear a friendly word of wisdom in a way we couldn't when we were in deep trouble.

This book is both the story about how I reached the limit of what I could handle and also about the ones who saw me through the most tumultuous time of my life. It's about both what went on during that year and my reflections on the meaning of it all after enough time had passed to allow me to recognize the gifts and graces of what I have come to call my "extraordinary time."

The key to my experience and its meaning is found in St. Paul's pastoral admonition to the Corinthians: "No testing has overtaken you that is not common to everyone. God is faithful, and he will not let you be tested beyond your strength, but with the testing he will also provide the way out so that you may be able to endure it."[1] What I have been pondering for more than two years now is that way out.

During the course of more than a year, from the spring of 2015 through the fall of 2016, I was taken time after time to the limits of my endurance and even of my life. Now I can see that this traumatic, fast-changing, almost surreal period was filled with mystery and redemption, loving presence and grace. Now, having been tested and refined from the fires of this intense period of adversity and slowly healing, I truly can say, gratefully, that God provided not only the way out but a particularly gracious way through it

---

1. 1 Cor 10:13. Unless noted, all biblical references are from the NRSV.

all. Like the Ancient Mariner in Coleridge's poem, who cornered anyone who would listen while he shared his eerie tale of testing, endurance, and survival through the grace of God, so too I feel compelled to share my extraordinary time so that others may be encouraged, consoled, and perhaps even inspired by my story.

Most of life is lived in what we might consider ordinary time, played out on the plains rather than the peaks and valleys. Thank goodness, as we could scarcely endure the constant ascending and descending, like on a roller coaster! I distinctly recall the one time I was persuaded to climb aboard such a scary ride, and once was enough! An occasional peak is nice, but otherwise I'm content to be a resident of the plains.

In the Christian church's liturgical calendar "ordinary time" is comprised of those long stretches between the major festivals from Advent to Epiphany and Lent and Easter to Pentecost. While the church doesn't name these peak seasons as "extraordinary time," they surely could be so considered, as their dramatic, earth-shaking events are compressed into a handful of days. Ordinary time both for the church and for each of us becomes the period following such intense, eventful times when we are able to step back, catch our breath, and reflect on what has happened, how it has changed us and our world, the mystery and the grace in it, and its implications for the future.

Although the dramatic events of my own recent extraordinary time provide the story line, recorded in Part 1, the heart of this book is my effort in Part 2 to reflect deeply and broadly on their meaning within the context of four great Christian themes: suffering, healing, death, and the afterlife. These themes are clearly interlinked: suffering leads either to healing or death—or healing through death—and death leads to the afterlife. How we are accompanied through our suffering, whatever the outcome, by our God and the Communion of Saints is a major focus of both parts. A reflection on the experience of death both from the perspective of those leaving their loved ones behind as well as the ones left grieving is explored in the chapter on death. The final chapter presents an in-depth inquiry into what awaits us after death, drawn from Scripture and the Christian tradition as well as experiential accounts of the afterlife. These four themes draw upon my own experience in conversation with the theology and practices of the Christian faith so that the one way of knowing illumines the other.

Suffering adversity is just part of the course of human life. As Christians, we should expect no less. After all, we follow the one who was crucified, so I don't claim that the events of my extraordinary time were any worse than what millions throughout the ages have suffered from natural disasters, wars, persecution, and personal traumas. But however common such occurrences may be, that doesn't make traumas less traumatic or suffering less painful. Because so much hit me in such a short period during which I was ill and vulnerable, the cumulative effects took me to the outer edge of my endurance.

Here is what happened: in the space of six months, I was faced with life-threatening colon cancer, major surgery to remove the cancer, chemotherapy with side effects so severe I couldn't complete the course of treatments, and the sudden death of my beloved husband. In the next few months, ongoing health issues from the chemo and then a fractured back left me incapacitated. Unable to keep my home in New Jersey and support my disabled son on the West Coast, I sold the house, disposed of treasured belongings, house-hunted on the other end, and, leaving my support system of family and friends behind, moved 2,700 miles across the country to Southern California. By any scale of measurement, the stress to my body, mind, emotions, and spirit from this accumulation of events was off the charts. The transition that began with my move to California, which was just about the last place I wanted to live and where I knew no one but my son, is the chapter of my story that is still unfolding.

Reflecting over the nearly three years since this extraordinary time began, I have come to see it as an extended near-death–like experience in which I was plucked from my ordinary life and suspended in an in-between, intermediate state on the threshold of death and the afterlife. What was happening in my three-dimensional world was very real, yet seemed overlaid by an otherworldly dimension through which I would catch an occasional glimpse of the meaning of what was going on and was able to recognize that I was being held within an embracing, ever-present field of love. Existing in this extended multi-dimensional state of being has given me a rare opportunity: to deeply experience the mysteries of suffering, healing, death, and the loving presences on both sides of a thin veil who accompany us through life's most dramatic, traumatic transitions.

A cancer survivor of more than two years now, I am hopeful that I will live at least a few more years. Although I'm fast approaching the three-quarters of a century mark, in prayer I have been given to believe that God isn't finished with me yet in this life. Nevertheless, I feel better prepared as a result of my recent experience to permanently cross over the threshold of death into the afterlife whenever God chooses to call me home. I am grateful for all that I experienced, for nothing that happened, even my husband's death, was without its gifts through the grace of God. While I may have experienced that second, deeper, and harsher "dark night of the spirit" about which the Carmelite mystic St. John of the Cross wrote five centuries ago, when God remains so hidden that we must trust in God's presence even when we feel God's absence the most, at no point did I feel truly abandoned or without hope. That was a huge grace before which I can only bow in thankfulness and humility.

As you will see, my life and reflections here have been deeply informed by Scripture, the Christian tradition, and its spiritual practices. A retired Presbyterian minister, oblate of a Benedictine monastery, and recent convert to Catholicism, my work now is teaching, leading retreats, and writing about Christian spirituality and spiritual formation. Earlier in the same year that I became Catholic, my last book, *Path of the Purified Heart: The Spiritual Journey as Transformation,*[2] was published and led to the founding of the ecumenical Friends of Christ School for Christian Spirituality in Chapel Hill, North Carolina, where I lived at the time. In the years since, my ongoing journey of transformation into ever deeper life in Christ has led me to places where despite my many years of religious formation I had not yet gone—or perhaps been willing to go.

By no means did I take this journey alone, although my inner experiences of it were uniquely mine. Truly, the only way out and through this extraordinary time was in the company of the great Communion of Saints. On this side of the veil these were family, friends, my monastic community and spiritual directors, church leaders and members of my parish, neighbors, and strangers who became friends—health care workers, real estate and estate sale agents, and interfaith volunteers. On the other side was a host of blessed beings—saints and saints in the making—with God in the realms of love and joy. One, my husband, began over here and crossed over there.

As a relatively new Catholic and a former academic, I have immersed myself in studying the Christian tradition in depth in order to find the language and metaphors to describe my own and others' experience and to deepen my spiritual practices of our faith. And as one who has been taken to the brink of death and beyond and is ready to welcome it, I find myself spending much time these days contemplating its mysteries and

2. Dunham, *Path of the Purified Heart,* Cascade, 2012.

those of the afterlife. One result of this extensive study and reflection is that I now view this liminal, intermediate state in which I have found myself for the past few years as my pre-death experience of purgatory, a subject of much controversy in the Christian tradition and much fascination as well. I am a willing participant in this final self-emptying and purifying stage of my spiritual journey toward God, and the more I allow and make room for Christ to dwell in me the more I appreciate the wisdom and beauty of God's judgment and mercy. I am exceedingly grateful to have been accompanied through this extraordinary time, as well as before and since, by the particular Communion of Saints that has gathered around me and those present of whom I have been unaware. They appear throughout this account as they appeared to me when I needed them and support me now on my continuing journey. This book is dedicated to them.

Most people of faith have not had the opportunity to explore in depth the four great themes presented here. My hope is that those who join me through Part 1 of this book on my perilous journey through extraordinary time will not only find deeper meaning in these explorations but also be better equipped through Part 2 to support others through suffering and healing and through death and renewed hope in the afterlife. Blessings on the journey!

Part 1: Extraordinary Time

ONE

Cancer and the Mysterious Free-Floating Cells

THE CALL CAME WHILE I was enjoying a delicious breakfast of *huevos rancheros* in the Plaza Diner in Santa Fe, New Mexico, where I had gone for a few days of retreat during Lent. My gastroenterologist's office confirmed the suspected diagnosis: colon cancer.

How could this happen? It had been about ten years since my last colonoscopy, so I was due, if not overdue, for one. No one likes going through this miserable procedure, let alone the two-day cleansing beforehand, but for the past few months I'd been having some rectal bleeding, not much, but often enough so that I needed to pay attention and have it checked out.

I had been feeling exhausted lately, very low on energy, but had attributed that both to my age—I'd just turned seventy-two—and the work I had taken on the previous fall and winter. I had been teaching all the religion classes for the upper-school girls at a local Catholic academy. Although I had enjoyed the girls and the subject matter, it took all my stamina to make it through each long day and keep up with four preparations, grading and recording assignments and tests, teachers' meetings, and the other duties of a full-time high school teacher. When the school day was over, I would go home to my husband, Alden, whose Parkinson's disease was progressively worsening, make sure he was cared for, feed and exercise Tyler, our sweet Golden Retriever, fix dinner, clean up the kitchen, and try to spend some time with Alden before heading to bed. After a semester of this routine, I wondered what I had been thinking when I agreed to fill in for a year until the school could find a more permanent teacher. I didn't feel well enough to complete the year, so arranged to leave at the end of the semester in January.

In February I resumed what had been my more normal, "ordinary time," routine: caring for Alden, managing the household, supporting my son Tom's care in the Los Angeles area where he was living in what was increasingly an untenable situation, and preparing for a retreat and classes I would offer during Lent. In addition to family visits, maintaining friendships near and far, and keeping up with email, this was more than enough for anyone my age, supposedly retired!

The rectal bleeding was daily now, and I visited my primary care physician who, somewhat alarmed, referred me to the gastro specialist. After meeting with him, which took less than five minutes, a colonoscopy was scheduled for early March. Following the procedure, while I was hoping to go home and have a good meal after two days of fasting, the gastro doctor sat me down and briskly informed me that I had an ulcerated colon with a hard mass, probably cancerous, and that a surgeon should be able to remove a section of the transept colon and repair it—if no lymph nodes were involved. Now he had my full attention. Had I heard it right? I sat there staring at him, trying to take this in. Cancer? Not me, surely! This wasn't supposed to happen. Later, I wondered if I had done something to cause this. Too much stress? Eating habits? Not enough exercise? Genetics? Searching for a reason, I remembered that my grandmother and a couple of aunts on my mother's side had died of what they called stomach cancer, but that was long ago and far away and couldn't be related to what was happening to me now. Could it? In shock from the news and the matter-of-fact way in which it had been delivered, I waited while the doctor ordered a CT scan for me later in the week and set up a meeting the following week with him and the surgeon he recommended.

Now I had to go home and break the news to Alden, then to Tom. Both would be upset and fearful, and I would have to reassure them that I would be okay, even if I wasn't sure of that myself. When you are caregiver to your closest loved ones, it often turns out that no one is available to take care of you when you need help. But both of them stepped up and were supportive, if anxious. As I notified close friends, other family, and my Benedictine community in Minnesota, people offered prayers and empathy. I was most grateful for how my own Communion of Saints, those people who cared about me, began to rally around from this point on with prayer and support.

The morning after the shocking news, I awoke, laid hands on my colon area, and prayed to Jesus for healing. For over fifteen years I had offered healing prayer and energy healing work for people, places, and situations in need. I had been mentored and trained by several gifted people of faith and for a number of years had trained others in what I considered this sacred work, often traveling on my own or with groups to offer healing where we were guided or sensed a need. The irony that I was now in need of major healing myself was not lost on me, but I trusted that whatever happened, all would be well. My years of spiritual practice and teaching had enabled me to detach from the outcome of what I was coming to view as "my cancer." Was it some alien, invading presence in my body that had grown, unbeknownst to me, in my colon and was about to break through the wall and take over my vital organs? Or was it something that grew from my own cells, taking shape from within my being, a dark expression of the shadow side of myself that was still evading God's generous love? Somehow I couldn't hate the tumor or see it as something to be attacked, as some who offered healing would advise, using visualizations of breaking up and defeating the enemy. I had never felt comfortable with the image of people who contracted cancer as "victims" or the obituaries which spoke of the deceased's "battle" with cancer. I didn't believe that this was the way of God. Healing was multi-dimensional, an interrelatedness of all dimensions of the self, not just the physical. It was God's loving us to wholeness, a state of being we will enjoy some time after death when, assured of God's promises of the resurrection of the dead, we are fully united with God. So I didn't want to think of cancer as an alien force that would destroy my body unless it was wiped out with deadly weapons. I wanted to love the cancer and to visualize it as just dissolving in the heat and light that flowed through me from God or as being transformed into healthy cells. But if that was not going to be the outcome, if it was not God's desire that I have the surgery and whatever other treatments might be necessary to preserve and prolong my life, then so be it.

Some years earlier I had completed the Ignatian Exercises, named after the sixteenth-century St. Ignatius, who founded the Jesuit order. These Exercises had deepened my relationship with Christ to such an extent that I took training in order to offer them to others. I was about to guide a group of women, most of whom worked in parish ministry, through a nearly eight-month journey through the Exercises, and it seemed prophetic that we would make this journey together, beginning now. If I was to be taken from this life by cancer, then I would welcome the stranger and offer it the fullest love of which I was capable. And I would pray from my heart the

Suscipe, prayed at the conclusion of the Ignatian Exercises, a prayer of utter surrender to God's desire for us: "Take, Lord, and receive all my liberty, my memory, my understanding, and my entire will, all I have and call my own. You have given it all to me. To you, Lord, I return it. Everything is yours; do with it what you will. Give me only your love and your grace; that is enough for me."[1]

At my best, that is what I was able to pray sincerely. But I wasn't always at my best. From the outset, I was more concerned about what would happen to Alden and Tom if I died first. For years I had suspected I might outlive them both, given their health issues. Whatever was God's desire for me was my desire for myself, but I fervently hoped and prayed that my two beloved men would not be put through the suffering of my death at this time. I knew that Alden would be cared for by the family. After all, we had moved back to New Jersey from Chapel Hill a couple of years previously so that he could spend his last years closer to his two sons, their wives, and the four local grandchildren. But Tom had no other family or even friends to turn to way out in California. Deep down I knew I needed to get through this ordeal, whatever it was, if for no other reason than to be there for my guys.

I had the CT scan the day before I was scheduled to leave for Santa Fe on private retreat. While there I planned to attend the graduation ceremony for my stepdaughter Carroll, who had completed her master's program at the Upaya Zen Center and was preparing to serve as a Buddhist chaplain. I saw no reason to cancel the trip, as I would meet with the doctors after I got back the next week. Alden would be looked after by the family. And Santa Fe was always a special place for me. On my first visit in 1987, I had fallen in love with its beauty and mystery and the way in which descendants of the conquistadors, Anasazi, and early Anglo settlers lived peacefully together. I had owned a vacation home there before Alden and I were married, and years later we had lived there for a time while I worked for a governing body of the Presbyterian Church in Arizona and New Mexico. Recently Carroll and her husband, Tom, a fifth-generation Santa Fean, had bought a condo there for times when they would return from their home in Nepal or from their many global travels to visit Tom's family. I had arranged to stay in the condo for the days of my retreat and was looking forward to just being in the high desert air and ambiance, along with visiting places I enjoyed in the area and meeting up with Carroll, whom we rarely saw.

1. Harter, ed., *Hearts on Fire*, 84.

It felt providential that I should be leaving for my beloved Santa Fe with a few days on retreat to begin to process the meaning of the life-threatening disease occurring at this time in my life and to pray for guidance on how to deal with it and all the ways it would disrupt our lives. I would also have an opportunity to revisit a well-known sacred site of healing in Northern New Mexico, El Santuario de Chimayo.

It was also providential that, when on my first day in Santa Fe the call came from the doctor's office to confirm the cancer diagnosis, I had already planned to spend the next day in Chimayo. The report was purely clinical: no empathetic physician calling to help me bear the bad news, only a staff member reporting that the tumor was 2.3cm/.9 inches around, in the ascending colon with no apparent liver involvement. I wondered how often the woman on the other end of the line had to make similar calls each day. At least at that point my tumor seemed confined to the colon. Returning to my now-congealed breakfast at the diner, the joy of the day as cold as the eggs, I thought about what I needed to do right away. Even though I was scheduled to meet with a general surgeon the following week, someone highly recommended who had done dozens if not hundreds of these surgeries, I wanted to meet with at least two oncologists who could assess the nature of the cancer and provide a follow-up plan. A few phone calls later, I had confirmed appointments with two of what would turn out to be four oncologists I consulted about my condition. Then I called Alden and his son, Ed, in case his father needed him. Both seemed to take the news as though I was delivering the weather report, so I knew neither was ready to take in fully its implications.

Meanwhile, poor Tom was having major dental surgery and was in great pain and trauma. He was upset that I was in New Mexico instead of seeing him through his ordeal. In retrospect, his was clearly the greater need, but then it almost always was. Gritting my teeth, I called yet another home health care agency to see if they could help out. I was assured someone would show up to spend the day with Tom. It was the best I could do at the moment.

Leaving the diner, I wandered around the plaza aimlessly for a while, seeing without noticing what I was looking at. Then, as it opened, I entered the nearby New Mexico History Museum to view a special exhibit, "Painting the Divine," featuring Marian art of the colonial period in the Southwest. As a new Catholic, I had devoted a couple of years to intentionally coming to know and love Mother Mary in ways that hadn't occurred to me or even been open to me as a Protestant minister. The devotion to Mary I saw in the paintings and carvings in the exhibit reminded me that the Mother of God and of the church was also my mother. Mary was a touchstone for me in my newly forming Communion of Saints. The beauty of each perspective on Mary reflected in the art was inspiring and comforting. I gave thanks to God for her and for this wonderful exhibit available to me when I needed a visible reminder of Mary's beautiful spirit and loving presence.

The rest of that day I went to familiar places for lunch and dinner, savoring the green Hatch chili that comes with nearly every New Mexican meal, and drove out to our old neighborhood and past the home where Alden and I had lived for several years. That feeling of being suspended in time and space began to surface in my awareness, and the whole experience felt surreal. I sensed that I no longer belonged in or to Santa Fe, or it to me. At the same time, the memories flooding in of past experiences I'd had with people I cared about when visiting each familiar place triggered a deep nostalgia and brought me to tears. It felt as if I'd lost something precious—a relationship with a land and its people, a deep bond. That night, grateful that I was alone to pray and process my feelings but bereft of human company, I went to bed early but didn't sleep well. My ears rang and my heart raced, and I wondered if these were caused just by the altitude of 7,000 feet or by what I now realized was a disease that could shorten my life. I thought about leaving early to return to the safety and comfort of my home and husband, but I wanted to attend Carroll's very special event and spend some time in her soothing company.

After breakfast the next day at another of my favorite Santa Fe eateries, I made the spectacular drive out to Chimayo, a tiny, dusty Northern New Mexican village washed in sunlight, which would be on few visitors' maps if it weren't for the Santuario. I had been there several times before and had brought back what was popularly believed to be miraculous healing dirt from a hole in the floor of one of the rooms off the chapel's nave. As a Catholic, I was learning to appreciate the place of sacramentals in our faith, those concrete sacred objects invested with holy meaning that we could see, smell, and touch. On the walls throughout the Santuario is the kitsch left by generations of visitors, chiefly cast-off crutches and braces from those healed in this sacred space, pictures of the healed, handwritten testimonials, and prayers of petition and thanksgiving. Numerous *milagros* dotted the walls: those little silver charms representing the parts of the body that received the healing, as though they were separable from the whole body: breasts, legs, feet, arms, and eyes were the most common *milagros*. I didn't see a colon there; if so, I would have bought one and carried it like a charm during the ordeals that were to come. Seriously. I would have, not believing it magical but rather imbued with the spirit of healing from that place and the prayers of those who sought such miracles.

For a time I wandered the rooms where people were gathering, most in silence. I scooped some dirt from one of the holes in the floor made by the faithful into a few bottles I bought for this purpose and sat praying for a while in the adobe chapel. I'm sure I asked for healing and for comfort for those most affected by my newly diagnosed disease, but for the most part I just wanted to rest in God in silent contemplation and feel loving presence.

On my way out, I ran into the resident priest-chaplain and asked if he would hear my confession. He was most willing to do so. Again, as a nearly lifelong Protestant whose tradition confesses only directly to God either privately or in corporate worship, I had to come to terms with confessing to a live priest, no longer in the traditional confessional booth where you are anonymous except to God, but face to face, knee to knee, and often in a not very private space. On this day I was most grateful for the encounter and the blessings of being confessed and of receiving God's guidance through this gentle priest. He said some helpful things, including something I pondered for some time afterwards: that I shouldn't expect myself to handle the cancer any better than I'd handled other challenges. And hopefully no worse, I thought. He told me not to be too hard on myself and instead of giving me penance laid his hand on my head, blessed and absolved me, saying that my sickness was penance enough and there was no need to do other penitential things. I was most grateful for my grace-filled encounter with this kind stranger, now enrolled in my Communion of Saints.

After staying for Mass, I wandered the grounds of the Santuario again, bought a candle and t-shirt in the gift shop, and treated myself to a lovely lunch at the very special Rancho de Chimayo restaurant nearby. Afterwards I drove slowly back to Santa Fe, enjoying the silence, rugged beauty, and peace of the countryside, which always lifted my heart and spirit. The excursion to Chimayo held at bay the anxiety which lurked beneath the surface of my being for those few, suspended-in-time hours.

Having worn myself out with all the stress and activity of the past couple of days, I slept well that night. The next day was Carroll's special event, and I joined her and her sister-in-law, Susan, at the graduation ceremonies, holy and beautiful in their own way. Upaya is one of those places you find around Santa Fe, where spiritual people, not always religious, gather. Their hospitality was lovely, and we enjoyed a vegan lunch before heading back into Santa Fe. The time with Carroll, who leads the most interesting life of anyone I know, was as always delightful. She and Tom and their two sons, Liam and Galen, live in Kathmandu, Nepal, but for many years have spent the summers on the Mongolian steppes, leading treks. Now they offer these for National Geographic, as well as jaunts to western Nepal, Bhutan, and other remote, exotic places. Carroll would play a large part later on in the drama of this extraordinary time, so you will meet her again, along with the rest of her family.

A couple of days later I returned home. The report from the gastroenterologist was in the mail. It seemed there were other conditions of the colon, along with the cancer, that would have to be addressed. The peaceful time in Santa Fe retreated into the distance, and my health issues took the foreground. Tom called to commiserate with me and to share his own miseries of extensive pain from the loss of his teeth and insufficient medication. His new caregiver was a no-show. This seemed to be a constant occurrence, no matter what the agencies promised. I was thrust rapidly back into my long-distance caregiver role for my son. Alden had fared all right, thankfully, and he and I kept the appointment with the surgeon.

The doctor said he would take up to ten inches of my colon with all the surrounding lymph nodes and blood vessels and told me that should be "curative" unless the cancer had invaded the lymph. I would be in the hospital for three to five days and convalescing at home for two to four weeks. The surgery would be done laparoscopically with three to four incisions, and he would repair my herniated belly button (news to me!) as a bonus. The other items on the gastro doctor's report he explained were age related and not too worrisome, so I parked those concerns for another day. It all seemed so straightforward and positive that I agreed on the spot to his doing the surgery. Its timing in late April would work out with my schedule. It gave me nearly a month to get everything in order.

I was nearly finished with offering a six-week class, "Lent with Mary," and had two other presentations scheduled before the surgery. I also had the group of five women to guide through the Ignatian Exercises over the next nearly eight months—which now seemed rather daunting—and we were to hold an opening retreat at a spirituality center on the beach in Cape May in a couple of weeks. Given what the surgeon had said, I didn't see any reason to cancel or postpone the Exercises. As it turned out, I was grateful for the group's regular presence in my life, and they were all added to my Communion of Saints.

I decided to consult another colon cancer specialist for a second opinion about my condition and the surgery and found this helpful. The doctor put me on medication for the ulcerative colitis, which I continued to take for a considerable time. I was advised to change my diet and eliminate nuts and seeds and red meat, all of which would irritate the colon even more. It was sinking in now that the cancer and surgery were more serious than I had been thinking and would involve significant lifestyle changes. I also began to speculate about my own role in contributing to the cancer in my body. Sugar and carbs, my two favorite food groups, could well have contributed to the problem, as well as being overweight with a low thyroid issue, which didn't help the situation. Neither did stress from the pressures of caregiving and concern about my loved ones and those I put on myself through my work and spiritual practices. I was reminded of what the Chimayo priest had said about my sickness being my penance and began to see its truth in a different light. *Mea culpa*, I prayed, asking for forgiveness for my part in harming the good body God had given me. Nevertheless, I continued to place my trust in God, to pray and to seek healing alternatives.

At the same hospital where the second doctor worked, I located a wonderful Franciscan sister, Sr. Pat, who soon became part of my Communion of Saints. The hospital had an alternative healing center which happened to be run by our granddaughter's mother-in-law. Sr. Pat was to offer me regular energy healing sessions during this entire time and even from a distance after my move. These were extremely helpful in keeping my energy balanced and offered much comfort. Several friends and family kept me in gift certificates for the treatments.

Meanwhile, a major tragedy occurred for my son. His beloved Siamese cat of sixteen years and his only companion, Loki, died suddenly. Tom was distraught. From across the country I was able to arrange for a pet cremation service that would pick up Loki's body and deliver his ashes to Tom. Who knew there were such services? I was most grateful for their help. The crises in my son's life would continue unabated during the time of my surgery and recovery and were just something I had to deal with. There weren't any alternatives that I could see, try as I might to find them. For the first time, I found myself considering sharing a home with Tom if something should happen to my husband. I doubted that I could maintain two households much longer, and Tom's needs were growing more critical. This thought became prophetic, as it turned out a year later.

Holy Week arrived. Usually I set aside most everything to be as fully present as I can to walk with Christ, the disciples, and Mother Mary through this holy time. But with all that was going on, I couldn't enter as fully into the sacred space of Maundy Thursday, Good Friday, Holy Saturday, or even Easter as I would have liked. I noted in my journal that it was a relief on Holy Saturday to have gotten through the pain, suffering, and agony of the cross. I had my own cross and Tom's to carry this year. Once again Tom's newly hired caregivers didn't show up, and he was suffering from severe anxiety. It seems that I have always taken my son's pain into my body since he was a child. When he was two and a half he slammed a door on his fingertip, almost severing it, just as my husband and I were leaving to attend the graduation ceremony in which I would receive my doctorate. Somehow it seemed as though Tom's crises happened at the worst possible times and trumped my own concerns. I often have thought that something synergistic goes on at times like these because of our strong energetic connection. Tom's disabling severe anxiety disorder and chronic pain left him with limited capacity to handle difficult situations on his own. For most of his adult life he had lived close by and at times with Alden and me. However, a year earlier he had wanted to move to the Los Angeles area and be on his own. He's a gifted musician who wanted to assemble an alternative rock band and create and perform music, something he had done in his youth and was still his dream. After much deliberation, we agreed to support his efforts. To do so from such a distance proved a greater challenge than I had anticipated, and managing his affairs as well as ours certainly amped up my stress levels.

A book I read recently by Gabor Maté, MD, *When the Body Says No: Understanding the Stress-Disease Connection*, confirms that severe, prolonged stress can manifest in the body in a variety of ways. Could mine have contributed to my cancerous tumor? By nature and inclination, I am an introverted contemplative who can spend hours alone reading and reflecting, thinking and praying, lost in that space between worlds. To be constantly or abruptly pulled out of these mental and spiritual states was and is stressful for me. I have had to learn to manage this over the years and had done so pretty well in my professional life, but now with Alden's decline, Tom's acute and chronic issues, and my own cancer, I had met my match. One issue relevant here and that would continue to arise even more after the move to California is this: which is my primary work? Is it staying in that contemplative space as fully present to God as I am able to be, or is it to be as present as possible in this world to the people God gave me to love and care for? Of course, the answer was both/and, not either/or, but I still seemed to give the greater share, at least emotionally and spiritually, to the contemplative in me. Was this of God or was it a form of escape from my other responsibilities? I would need to reflect much more deeply on this central question in the days to come.

Unable to attend the Easter Vigil, always the highlight of the Christian year for Catholics, I stayed home and rested but did manage to get to the Easter morning Mass. Having missed out on several of the special liturgies of Holy Week made my experience of it this year feel disjointed. Yet because it was a time of great chaos and uncertainty in the lives of the disciples, I felt closer to their experience of Jesus' passion than ever before. One powerful image that came to me during this season and has stayed with me ever since is that of the *pieta*, the shocking, pitiable state of Mary's holding her lifeless son in her lap after his broken body had been removed from the cross. In my presentations on "Lent with Mary" I had pulled together a number of great artists' portrayals of the *pieta*. For many years I have had in my prayer room a replica, which had been my mother's, of Michelangelo's famous *Pieta* in St. Peter's Basilica. But this year I was drawn more to one of Bellini's stark images, with Mary standing next to the gruesome, tortured body of her son, holding him up. It was excruciating, almost unbearable for me to look at, as I thought of how my own son suffered. The artist elicits great pity for Mary in her desolation and sorrow but also reveals her strength and courage. Despite the joy of Easter with its promise of new life with Christ and the glorious future when all will be united on heaven and earth through him, this year I couldn't go there. I was drawn into the intensity of Christ's suffering and that of those who loved him most. As I prayed for my husband and son, I lifted them to Christ as though I had been holding them on my own lap, like Mary. This has become a common prayer practice for me, especially for those for whom I have the greatest concern.

Following Easter, I returned to my work schedule, spending the weekend in Cape May with the Ignatian group to launch them on their journey through the Exercises. Next up was giving a presentation at St. Mary's Abbey in Morristown, New Jersey, where oblates of the three Benedictine communities in the state had gathered for their annual meeting. My presentation was on ongoing oblate formation, something I had also spoken about at the American Benedictine Academy convention the previous year, and care deeply about. Both of these gatherings went well, but I was exhausted when they were over.

With these obligations met, it was now time to prepare for the surgery to remove my cancerous tumor. I knew that many in my Communion of Saints were praying for me, and that gave me strength and comfort. My good friend Christine came by and gifted me with a first-class relic of St. Elizabeth Ann Seton, the first canonized native-born American and founder of the Sisters of Charity of Saint Elizabeth, whose Mother House is in Convent Station, New Jersey. One of the living sisters had given it to Christine, who generously passed it on to me. I treasure this sacred remnant of a saint I greatly admire, and carried the relic with me to the hospital, along with other sacred objects.

The day of the surgery came all too soon. I felt enveloped in prayer as I entered the operating room and was ready to have the cancer removed and to get on with my life. Hours later, as I awoke from the anesthesia, I was told the surgery had gone well and that the doctor had removed about ten inches of my colon and attached appendix along with nineteen lymph nodes. That sounded like a lot of lymph nodes to me, but they cautiously take as many as could possibly have been breached by the cancer. I was told that the tumor was still contained within the wall of the colon but was close to breaking through, in which case it would have metastasized throughout my body. It would take a few days for the biopsies to come back to ensure that they had gotten all the cancer. I hoped and prayed that the surgery was, indeed, "curative," as my surgeon had suggested it would be.

Meanwhile, grateful to have this crucial stage of my recovery behind me, I rested as much as one can while spending four days in the hospital. I had a good number of visitors—family, friends, the priest from my parish and other friends from church—along with many comforting messages. At times like these, the great cloud of witnesses who gather around us in heaven and on earth are deeply felt and appreciated.

After a few days my bowels started to work again, and I was able to go home. But not all was well in my world. Carroll and her family in Nepal had suffered through an earthquake of historic dimensions. Devastation was everywhere, but thankfully they were safe. Our grandson Liam, then nineteen, accompanied his photojournalist father to document the destruction and assist in locating survivors. He saw a great deal of death firsthand. And my Tom was not doing well after dental surgery and needed care. Did his concern over my illness amplify his own? It certainly contributed to his level of anxiety. Throughout that trying time Tom's concern for me mirrored mine for him. We were drawn together, it seemed, in a kind of morphic resonance, a united field of energy where we felt each other's pain, which amplified when we did so, almost as though in a continuing spiral.

My friend Christine had also been discovered to have a form of cancer and was scheduled for surgery a week after I got home. What was going on? Couldn't the world around me stay calm while I recovered? I wasn't able to really be there for Christine in her surgery and recovery other than through prayer and loving support, but I had no choice at that point. Fortunately, her surgery turned out well, and later we were able to celebrate a clean biopsy and a good prognosis.

My report, however, was not as bright. The surgeon called with mixed news on results of the biopsies. He had removed nineteen lymph nodes, and a few cancer cells were found floating in one of them. He wasn't sure what this meant but advised me to consult an oncologist about possibly following up with chemotherapy. Needless to say, this was disturbing news. The surgery hadn't quite been curative. Now what? What to make of those few cells became a major mystery. Over the next couple of weeks I was to research extensively the pros and cons, ins and outs of chemotherapy, especially the question of whether or not it would substantially increase the odds that I would live longer than five more years. I ended up consulting no fewer than four oncologists with differing opinions and counsels, even regarding what stage of colon cancer I had, Stage 2a or Stage 3. The odds of survival differed depending on which stage they believed I had. I learned that I was at high risk for another cancer. Chemo would improve the odds of my longer-term survival by about 5 percent, not a huge difference. Even afterwards, there's a 10 to 25 percent chance of a recurrence.

One oncologist practiced in a group connected with the hospital closest to my home. She advised against chemo. The second practiced in a private facility about forty minutes away not connected with a hospital. He advised for chemo. We lived in central New Jersey with a prestigious medical school and hospital at the nearby University of Pennsylvania in Philadelphia. I was blessed to get an early appointment with a colon cancer specialist there who basically said there would not be much benefit to chemo. The odds didn't substantially increase that it would extend my life by killing off any potential remaining cancer cells, and that I could take it or leave it. That left me in a quandary. There was no consensus. Should I go the conservative route and subject myself to months of harsh, toxic chemo which would destroy healthy cells along with any remaining cancer, or should I take my chances and assume I was cured?

These confusing consultations left me with an excruciating decision to make about whether or not to undergo chemotherapy. I truly felt obligated to stick around for as long as Alden was alive and hopefully for long enough to see some improvement in Tom's condition and quality of life. No one else in Tom's life was prepared to take over his care. I also enjoyed my work, relationships, and communities, and would not mind continuing to live as long as God allowed. I was engaged in the kind of discernment I had learned from both the Benedictine and Ignatian traditions: a process of deep listening and sorting through options, evidence, and clues for where God was in this matter of my life or death, in order to make a decision that would accord with where the Holy Spirit was leading me. At this point I felt the need for a final opinion and elected to see one more colon cancer expert at another reputable facility, the Fox Chase Cancer Center in Philadelphia. I sent my medical records ahead of my appointment, including the slides of the biopsies requested, noting that no one else had looked at these. The doctor and team with whom I met at Fox Chase felt that because there had been those few free-floating cancer cells in one of the removed lymph nodes my cancer was not Stage 2a, where chemo was more optional, but rather Stage 3, where the odds of survival improved from a 5 percent margin of life expectancy gained to double that percentage or more. In other words, the worse the stage, the more likely chemo would improve the odds that I would survive more than five more years. He urged me to consider undertaking the treatment every other week over about six months for a total of twelve infusions. It made me queasy to think about this, but I respected the doctor and was inclined to trust his counsel. But first I wanted to prayerfully consider my options, along with the different doctors and facilities, before arriving at a decision.

Mother's Day came and went, with nice visits, phone calls, and messages, then Ascension of the Lord, a Holy Day of Obligation for Catholics. I was able to attend Mass and to reflect on the mystery of Christ's ascension, an essential part of the post-Easter to Pentecost season, yet not much celebrated or well understood in the church. If Christ doesn't ascend after his post-resurrection appearances, how does the church understand his place in the universe and the life of the world to come? Part of my role in teaching adult spiritual formation, I felt, was to help people learn the meaning and significance of the sacred mysteries and liturgies of our faith.

My discernment continued. Alden's and my twenty-sixth wedding anniversary came around. We celebrated with dinner at our favorite local diner. We had made it longer than we might have anticipated, given our nearly twelve-year age difference and the now thirteen years since his diagnosis of Parkinson's disease. I wondered if this would be our last anniversary, if one or the other of us would depart before the next one came around. Sadly, this proved a prophetic thought.

That same week I took my husband for another surgery on his drooping eyelid. The hope was that it would improve both his vision and his looks. A handsome, physically fit man, a fine tennis player most of his adult life, he had struggled for years emotionally as well as physically with his body's deterioration from both the Parkinson's and arthritis. His intellectual decline was also evident to us both. With three Ivy League degrees (and an honorary doctorate, he would want me to add) and a distinguished career as a foundation executive who had had a major impact on American higher education over the years, Alden now had to come to terms with a much diminished life and constant, chronic pain. If the eyelid surgery would lift his spirits, I was all for it.

Alden's older daughter, Ellen, a professor of architecture and urban design at Georgia Tech, came for a visit, and I felt it was time to seriously consider long-term care options for him, particularly if my recovery didn't go well. Although he had fallen a few times in the past year, he hadn't required hospitalization. But I sensed that we needed to be prepared for the possibility that he wouldn't be mobile enough much longer for me to cope with his care on my own. This common concern for people with aging or disabled family members also was a matter of faith for me. We were committed to each other for better or for worse. Worse had arrived. The most loving option in my view was to care for my husband at home until his death or my incapacity. It seemed, however, as though both were approaching, and we needed a Plan B. We began to explore two possibilities: an assisted living facility nearby or a home health care agency to help with daily living. Neither seemed a good fit. The facility cost was prohibitive, at least as long as I was alive and living independently. Home health care might help during the day, but what if he fell at night or needed help getting to the bathroom? I was grateful for Ellen's caring, level-headed participation in the exploration of how her father's coming needs might be met, as I was more aware of my own limited life expectancy and good health after what I had just gone through. But much worse was to come.

As the days passed and I continued to heal from the surgery, it was time to make a decision about chemotherapy. After much prayer and consideration, I chose to go ahead with chemo at Fox Chase. The decision was to try to improve the odds that I would be around to support my husband and son, despite the risks. After getting a mammogram to ensure I didn't currently have breast cancer, a date was set for me to have a port installed in my chest at Fox Chase to receive the chemo injections. It was all becoming too real too fast.

A few days before the port procedure was Pentecost, the coming of the Holy Spirit to the apostles, one of the great festivals of the church. I prayed that the fresh winds of the Spirit would blow through our world—my world—bringing new life and hope, faith, and love to all of God's creation and to me and my beloveds.

TWO

Chemo and the Mysterious Gene Mutation

THE MYSTERY OF THOSE pesky free-floating cancer cells had not really been adequately explained in my view. One oncologist was of the opinion that they would probably be killed off by my body's immune system after the surgery. The one I chose to listen to was of the worst-case opinion, that they were a sign the cancer had spread outside the colon and should be destroyed by the chemo before they did any more damage. I still don't know who was right. Only God knows. But I found it ironic that I was about to poison my body and kill off millions of healthy cells when I might not even have cancer any longer!

Since I made the decision to go ahead with the chemo, I have resisted trying to second-guess it but rather to own it, as I reached it through the prayer process of discernment. Part of that process is observing how you feel about each option (consolations and desolations, pros and cons), and praying hard until the choice or outcome which you believe to be closest to God's desire for you is as clear as it's going to be by the time you have to act. I chose to subject myself to the poisonous toxins of the chemical mix that would be pumped into my body in order to try to extend my life expectancy primarily for the sake of my husband and son. I suspect most others in similar circumstances would have done the same. I entrusted my life to God for real. Little did I know I would soon go into free fall.

A few years ago I lost a dear friend to cancer. Meg had decided not to endure chemo. A health educator and healer, she didn't want those toxins killing off her healthy cells along with the cancerous ones. She tried alternative treatments, but it soon became clear that she had run out of

19

time. Single with no children, Meg felt free to choose how to leave because no one other than her close friends and a sister depended on her sticking around, and we didn't have a vote. She handled all her affairs with her usual competence, distributed gifts and personal effects to friends, and graciously invited us, one by one or in groups, to spend her last days with her to share loving memories and bless her on her way. She taught me much about how to die well, as I share more fully later on. Meg left us the day after her sixtieth birthday on Epiphany. To me, her passing paralleled the journey of the wise ones home after receiving the light of Christ.

Although I chose to stay and try to extend my life, as it turned out the treatment proved to be at least as deadly as the disease. What we didn't know when we started the course of chemotherapy was that I had a mysterious genetic mutation that, had it gone undiscovered much longer, would have taken my life.

There is only one standard protocol for colon cancer treatment and, believe it or not, it was developed over fifty years ago! That astonished me. With all the research on cancer and the promising new drugs and treatments, like immunotherapy that targets only the cancer cells in your body, my protocol had to be older than any other, it seemed. Later, Tom would tell me that the chemicals used were developed for mustard gas in World War I. I didn't want to know that, but after enduring this treatment I could believe it. My extraordinary time was beginning in earnest.

At the end of May I put myself into the capable hands of the medical staff at Fox Chase. Christine, who became a stalwart and dear companion through the months ahead, took me down to Philadelphia for the blood work, CT scan, and installation of the port. Ports are plastic, quarter-sized devices inserted under the skin in the upper chest attached to a vein and a catheter. The chemo cocktail and whatever other drugs the patient is to be given are delivered through a needle inserted into the port. Without one, you would be stuck each time by intravenous needles in your arm or hands. I know, it makes me queasy, too. You have no idea. I'm someone who looks away when my blood is drawn and thinks of anything else. Majorly squeamish, that's me. When I was going off to college in the sixties, there were only two professions into which women were generally accepted: teaching or nursing. Nursing was definitely out, so I became a teacher like my mother. See how I've diverted attention away from the needles and the port? The procedure of installing the port under light anesthesia supposedly went well, but the site bled long afterwards and hurt the entire time I had it in my upper chest, making it hard to sleep on that side of my body. Still, I was grateful not to have to be stuck every single time, because the chemo treatment always started with blood work. Vials of blood would be drawn and sent to the in-hospital lab so that my doctors could check my levels before ordering the amount and mixture of chemo I would receive that day. The port sometimes got clogged, but I will spare you those details.

A few days after the port installation, June 4, as a matter of fact, I was scheduled for my first chemo treatment. Christine's husband, Chick, would drive me down to Fox Chase, and later Christine would pick me up. It's not advisable that patients drive themselves because of all the side effects, including nausea and dizziness. These turned out to be the least of my symptoms, as you will see.

The word *patient* gives me pause. Being a patient seemed to have become my primary role. I don't know why that word is used but maybe because if you are not a patient person when you start this process, you had better be one by the time you finish, or you will lose your mind. When you are a patient you are no longer in control of your life. You are at the mercy not only of God, which you want to be, but of the medical system, the meds you are given, and your caregivers. Also, the long hours that the treatment took each time and the aftereffects, which lasted for days, were an endurance test. Being patient was essential to being a chemo patient. Patience is one of the highest of the spiritual virtues, I'm convinced, and, since I had not learned to practice it sufficiently by then, I was given a more advanced opportunity.

Being picked up and delivered by friends or family for my treatments became a pattern. Alden could no longer drive, so I had to arrange rides each time. People were gracious, and, as it turned out, Interfaith Caregivers, a local volunteer agency, provided strangers for many of my rides who became some of the gifts of this time. All have special places in my Communion of Saints.

I would be picked up at home on the day of treatment and deposited at Fox Chase. There I would check in and wait to be called for my blood work, which had to be completed at least an hour before the infusion was scheduled, in order to allow the labs to process and report the blood count to the doctors. After that wait, most days I would go down to the doctors' area and wait to see them. We would meet for a few minutes to nearly an hour, depending on what had happened since the last treatment. And an awful lot happened. After that I might get something to eat and then would wait again, practicing patience until it was my turn to be called into the infusion room.

What I am about to describe to you helps explain why I now believe that purgatory happens, for the most part, during this life rather than in the afterlife, at least for those of us on an intentional spiritual journey toward union with God. I'll fill in the details later. For now, just take my word for it. Remember Dante's *Inferno,* where those who enter hell pass under a sign advising the new residents to abandon all hope? The sign on the door to the infusion room should say, "Welcome to Purgatory. Hold on to your hope. You'll need it in here."

The infusion room is where cancer patients sit side by side in recliners in a circle around the perimeter of this large space. I noticed after a while that none of them would talk to each other, only occasionally to whoever came with them, or to the medical staff. That puzzled me. After a few times there I figured out that people were just too tired and sick to make the effort. Besides, I don't think they wanted to hear about each other's ailments. All they could deal with at the time were their own and getting through another treatment.

First we—because I'm now one of them—receive our anti-nausea meds through our ports along with any other meds our doctors prescribe. After those have slowly dripped into our veins, the entree is served: a toxic chemical cocktail prepared especially for each patient-guest, depending on the kind of cancer you have and how much you can tolerate. Several hours later, when the drip bags are empty, you are disconnected and free to go home. I always bolted for the bathroom first, after receiving so many liters of liquids.

While all this is going on people doze, watch TV on little individual screens attached to their recliners, snack on soda crackers and juice delivered periodically by friendly volunteers, or doze. I seemed to be the only one who read. I loaded my iPad with light reading that would distract me from what was being emptied into my body, like New Mexico mystery series or the Brother Cadfael novels set at a Benedictine monastery in medieval England. At times I would look up to observe that the other patients just stared blankly ahead. Were they contemplating their fate? Some looked really sick—thin, losing their hair, sunken eyes, pallor or gray-looking skin. Welcome to purgatory!

While most patients were unhooked from their IVs at the end, I was rehooked to a bottle resembling a thermos in a nylon cover that contained all the chemo that would be slowly dripping into me over the next day and a half. I would strap this bottle around my waist. It went everywhere with me. After it was finally empty I either would have to return to Fox Chase to have it removed or get someone with the courage to unclip the large needle from my port to do it for me at home. Thanks be to God, our daughter-in-law Wendy, made of sterner stuff than I, agreed to let the nurses at the cancer center train her in this procedure. She went down there with me the first couple of times, then bravely took over the process, which spared me a great deal of stress and travel. Wendy, a special education teacher, would have made a good nurse. She truly belongs in my Communion of Saints!

If my description of these treatments sounds routine, the results definitely were not. The day after my first infusion was the twenty-first anniversary of my ordination as a Minister of Word and Sacrament in the Presbyterian Church (USA). The occasion and the anniversary mean a great deal to me, even though I had to lay aside my ordination when I joined the Catholic Church. I still wear what I consider my ordination ring, inscribed with "Be Thou My Vision" and the date: June 5, 1994. Even though I was well into my forties in 1991, I know that God called me into the ministry. I had experiences and confirmations that were unmistakable, even though I didn't know much about discernment back then. I served in pastorates in South Carolina and Georgia and later retired from a position with a governing body of the church in the Southwest. That's when we lived in Santa Fe. As anyone who knows people in religious life can confirm, ministers, priests, and the religious don't ever really retire. We just change the nature and the place of our ministries. And I firmly believe that, unless we seriously violate our vows, once we are ordained we remained ordained in God's eyes, if not always those of the church.

Usually on that anniversary I spend time in prayer and contemplation, reflecting on the graces of my service in the church, but this day I didn't feel at all well. Although I had been given anti-nausea meds, along with Prednisone, a steroid I really don't like, I felt nauseous and hadn't been able to sleep. A day later I was still nauseous and had no appetite. I was able to eat only simple food, like a boiled egg, toast, and that perennial childhood favorite, chicken noodle soup. Digestive issues added to my misery. I was too sick to go to church on Sunday, so I prayed the office of the Mass at home. I wasn't able to read, so now I began spending most of my time either in the upholstered chair in my study/prayer room listening to sacred music or lying in bed watching Hallmark Channel movies, HGTV, or a

Tigers' baseball game, although that often proved more vexing than the other channels, which usually put me to sleep. I began to notice something that would continue throughout my extraordinary time. My world began to shrink down to the size of my own needs. When we are sick we can't do much more than stay in the present moment or slip into that liminal state between waking and sleeping.

In the meantime, life was going on around me. Alden needed to eat, have his laundry done, his meds picked up at the pharmacy, and, most of all, company during the long hours of the day. I wasn't very good company during these months, sad to say. But other members of the family were around to pitch in. Ed took his dad back to the eye doctor to get his eyelid re-stitched, and his married daughter, Kate, would stop by with our new great-grandson, Max. Occasionally someone would drop off a much appreciated meal. A woman from Interfaith Caregivers came over to assess my needs for help from their agency, and Meals on Wheels started the process of getting Alden enrolled for a daily hot meal. These agencies' services proved to be a great help during the coming weeks.

One week after the first chemo treatment, the nausea and sick feeling still continued. Most days I could barely get out of bed, but I had to take Alden to a major appointment with his Parkinson's doctor, which led to his reluctant agreement to start a mobility program at the nearby hospital. I also took him to get his hair washed and cut and to the podiatrist for toenail trimming. Even though it exhausted both of us, I was grateful for these services, routine for many elderly.

One day in prayer I heard, "You are God's anointed." It reassured me of God's loving care of me. My heart filled with gratitude for all the blessings being showered on me through prayer and presence. I was also beginning to learn one of the huge lessons and gifts of this time: to receive with grace and gratitude. Those of us who have spent much of our lives caring for others are used to giving. Those in the professional ministry often become workaholics. Self-care, giving to the self, and being able to graciously receive from others what they are lovingly offering, are often underdeveloped in people like me. Was my illness the result of my own incapacity to balance giving with self-care and gracious receiving? Someone told me around this time that colon cancer was a metaphor for holding anger and resentment deep in our guts rather than processing it and releasing it from our energy fields. Was I guilty of this? Did I resent my caregiving roles for Alden, Tom, and others? At some level, I believed I did. It was time for me to pray and reflect more deeply on this physical-emotional-spiritual connection. As I began to realize how much I was receiving from so many people, I began to appreciate the kindness, generosity, and love that is available to us through our Communion of Saints if we will allow them to bless us as they would gladly do. I knew the joy of giving. Now it was time to learn the joy of receiving.

Two weeks after the first treatment, after being sick the whole time, even feverish, I returned to Fox Chase. My doctors were alarmed and called off the second infusion because of a low white cell count. Mine was only 600 and should have been over 1,000. I had what they called neutropenia. My count was so low my body couldn't fight infection. I went over my other symptoms with them, and they told me to come back in a week.

At home I began running a fever. Family and friends showed up to help with meals and Alden's care. By June 21, the summer solstice, my white cell count had dipped dangerously low to 328. My doctors ordered me hospitalized. I chose to be admitted into the medical center just a few minutes from our home rather than in Philadelphia, so that Alden and others could visit. Even the priest from my parish came, although he didn't give me the sacrament of the Anointing of the Sick, which I would have welcomed. That sacrament may be received any time someone is ill and in need of healing. Not since Vatican II fifty years ago had it been considered "Last Rites" for the dying. Those couple of days in the hospital I received infusions of heavy-duty antibiotics. When my count gradually moved up to 728, I was released to come home. Rob, Alden's younger son, a Colonel in the Air Force Reserves, was kind enough to take a half a day off to pick me up. He had spent some time with his dad as well, who naturally was very upset about what was happening with me. A day later was Father's Day, and Alden was taken to Ed and Wendy's home for a celebratory dinner with the whole family. I was glad for him but sorry I couldn't join them.

By that time I was just home recovering. My temperature returned to normal, but I was very weak and exhausted. My hair had begun to fall out every time I passed a comb or brush through it. That wasn't supposed to happen in this time-tested colon cancer chemo protocol. I'm not vain about my hair, which has been quite short most of my life, but going bald was not on my radar screen. I began to empathize with Tom, who had suffered from hair loss for years. Nothing was going as expected with this chemo protocol. I was starting to become anxious about my prognosis and whether or not I should continue the treatments.

Given all this, I figured I had better move ahead with consulting an estate planning attorney to update our wills. Alden and I talked about what we wanted changed, including the need for a trustee for the trust to be set up for Tom in the event of our deaths. This would require special arrangements not easily accomplished.

As the days passed, a number of concerned people checked in with me, including two good friends, Ann Marie and Theresa, my spiritual director, from St. Benedict's Monastery, the place of my oblate affiliation. I managed to keep up with the Ignatian group making the Exercises, even meeting them for lunch one day, and to take Alden to his workout sessions. Poor Tyler, our Golden Retriever, then seven years old, wasn't getting enough exercise. I couldn't walk him anymore, as I had usually done, so he had to make do with running around our yard and barking at the dogs next door. Tyler is definitely a part of the Communion of Saints. In fact, he's an angel in a furry disguise. He rarely left my side when I was home and suffered along with me. A friend who met him years ago dubbed him Tyler, Prince of Dogs. That suited him.

I was scheduled for my next chemo treatment on July 2, four weeks after the first. What a four-week period that had been! I was quite apprehensive about what would happen this next time. Interfaith Caregivers had lined up a driver for me who would take me down to Fox Chase and wait to bring me back, making a very long day for both of us. David turned out to be another great gift of this time. He was not only accommodating and helpful but an interesting conversation partner. A practicing Baha'i, a religion that emphasizes the union and equality of all people, David and I had long discussions about our respective faiths and spiritual practices, and I grew to look forward to those times when he was my driver and companion. Communion of Saints? Definitely!

During my next doctors' appointment at Fox Chase I learned something of huge significance to my treatment. Through blood testing, it was discovered that I have a rare genetic mutation known as DPD (short for Dihydropyrimidine Dehydrogenase—I can't pronounce it, either), which in 5 percent of colon cancer patients makes the Folfox chemo protocol toxic and potentially fatal! The markers of the anomaly were, not surprisingly, hair loss and neutropenia.

One might well ask why this mutation isn't routinely tested for before patients are given the regime, but you might also suspect the answer: it's a very expensive set of tests for which Medicare and health insurers don't like to pay. So I was given a potentially fatal drug, and, instead of saving money, my insurers had to spend thousands of dollars for the cost of my hospitalization from neutropenia and the additional after-effects!

At this point I could only be grateful that this deadly anomaly was discovered before it was too late. It made my choice of oncologists providential, as I doubt that the first two I had visited would have discovered the anomaly or caught it as quickly as my colon cancer specialist. Nevertheless, it was greatly concerning. The doctors decided to cut back on the doses of the two drugs, to titrate them in order to find out how much I could tolerate. They wanted the treatment to be as effective as possible without killing me. Sounded like a plan to me! However, it would be an experiment for all of us, and my case had them baffled throughout, I believe, not only because of the DPD but also my hypersensitivity to medications and procedures. I don't think that is uncommon for those of us who have meditated and cleared and balanced our energy fields for many years. Quite a few people I have met through spirituality and healing work do not do well on typical protocols and medications. That includes my son, Tom, who has proven to be a challenge to just about every doctor who has tried to treat him. That's part of the reason why he is disabled and needs care.

For my second treatment, my doctors reduced one part of the dose by 50 percent, quite an enormous amount, and the other by 20 percent. In the coming months, they would titrate down considerably more, as I consistently was unable to tolerate the amount of the last dose. That day proved a very long one, and I didn't get home until 7:30 PM. Friends of Alden's from his workout facility had kindly dropped off a hot meal, along with their good company. For my part, I collapsed in bed and didn't even need *House Hunters* to put me to sleep.

The fourth of July came, with another family gathering at Ed and Wendy's. These opportunities to be with family were the primary reason I had felt guided to move us back to New Jersey in 2013, just in time for Kate's wedding. Alden enjoyed being around the family very much, even though he couldn't take part in the conversations or activities as he used to. Ed faithfully came for him almost every Saturday morning and took him to breakfast and errand-running. Later, Ed and Wendy would pick him up for church. Since I had become Catholic, Alden was without a church home, but he found one in the small Lutheran Church that Ed's family belonged to. He liked the pastor and the sermons. I was glad for that, especially in light of what lay ahead.

I remained sick, with nausea, diarrhea, and exhaustion. My best friend from high school and college, Pat, called me from Milwaukee to commiserate. That made my day. There's nothing like having a great old friend who knows everything about you and still loves you. We got into some escapades together during our teenage years and enjoyed laughing about those together. She and Tom are two of the few people who can make me really laugh. Alden used to say that I have an underdeveloped sense of humor, but I think it's just that I don't find humorous anything that puts down people or animals, and that eliminates most of the sitcoms on TV.

Alden's eighty-fourth birthday came around on July 9. Friends and family called or sent messages, including Carroll and Tom from Mongolia, where they spend their summers. I took him to our local diner for lunch, a treat for both of us, and Wendy brought over a cake. He had a nice day. I was glad in retrospect, as it was to be his last birthday.

St. Benedict's Feast Day happens on July 11, and I prayed with gratitude for my Benedictine sisters at St. Ben's. I had been used to getting up to St. Joseph, Minnesota to spend a week or so with them a couple of times a year, but I was unable to go at all during this entire span, and so had to make do with phone calls, email, an occasional Skype call, and lots of prayers back and forth.

My condition continued to deteriorate. Rectal bleeding continued, even after the surgery. I saw my primary care doctor, who said it was more ulcerative colitis but that no procedures or treatments could be done because they could cause infection due to the neutropenia. That was to be the case for nearly the next two years, as I slowly recovered from the ravages of the chemo to my body.

After another consult, my doctors confirmed that I am unable to metabolize the chemo mix. They cut the dose by 20 percent more and said they would keep an eye on the results and titrate more if need be. One scary thought was that, however reduced, the chemicals could still have very severe consequences as they accrued in my body.

I continued to be sick and exhausted. My parish held an Anointing of the Sick sacrament that I wasn't going to miss. I was grateful for it, and for the visiting priest who advised me to bring my weakness and pain to Christ on the cross. Like Therese of Lisieux, the nineteenth-century Carmelite, who mastered this kind of prayer, I wanted Jesus to transform my suffering into healing for others.

Our granddaughter, Kacie, then a rising sophomore at Vanderbilt, stopped by for a welcome visit. We hadn't seen much of her since she left for college. Christine's birthday the same day called for a special lunch, so I took her out. I was glad for the opportunity, but it was too much for one day for me. I was rapidly discovering my limits.

For the third chemo treatment, David took me down and Ellen, who was visiting, picked me up. It was a delight to have her around. I talked through the estate plans and options for her father's care if I should go first with her. Friends from Chapel Hill stopped by on their way home from travel. We were being visited by our Communion of Saints quite regularly during this period, which we both much appreciated.

Two weeks later I managed to tolerate the fourth chemo. Meanwhile, I arranged for the outside of our house to be painted and an appraisal to be done in case we had to sell. This proved to be another insightful decision.

Tom had been trying to keep me from worrying about him, but his situation wasn't improving, either. His dental surgeon wouldn't prescribe painkillers for him any longer, and Tom was suffering. The dentist told him to go to the emergency room. Tom refused. I had arranged for him to move at the end of the month to a smaller apartment in his complex to save money. How would he manage? Tom made the decision to go to a clinic that would help him get off the painkillers. I was pleased that he had taken this crucial step but quite worried about him. He needed more care and guidance than I was able to give or provide at that time.

The day of my fifth treatment, not only was Tom in pain, but Alden fell in the bathroom and, as they say in the ads, couldn't get up. This was alarming to us both. Was this the beginning of the end? I was home when it happened but well might not have been. It took me ten minutes to help him move to a sitting position where he could use the leverage of the bathtub to raise himself. I went to chemo anyway and let the family know what had gone on. The mental and emotional pain I suffered along with my husband and son began to take its toll.

After Labor Day I met with the estate planning attorney and got the process of updating our wills moving along. Someone needed to be named as a trustee for Tom's trust. Christine seemed the perfect choice. After prayer and consideration, she agreed. I was greatly relieved. She knew what she was taking on but agreed to do it anyway. I was and am most grateful for this generous, loving friend.

Sensing that things were about to change, when I felt up to it I cleaned out my clothes closets and got rid of a ton of things that were just taking up space. Ed kindly came and took them to the Goodwill. I may not have fully realized it at the time, but I was already preparing for the transition that lay ahead and would transform all our lives.

The sixth and seventh chemo treatments came and went. The doctors lowered my dose another 20 percent as I wasn't tolerating the chemicals well. It seemed to me that I was down to no more than about 10 to 15 percent of what the original dose had been and was still getting sick. They told me that if I continued to have side effects, they could either stretch out the treatments or stop them.

Carroll flew over from Nepal and came to town for a long overdue visit. It was a delight, as always, to see her. She pitched in with the program, picking me up at Fox Chase one day, taking her father to the dentist the next, helping me get stuff out of the basement into the garage for pickup from AmVets. She took her father to his next Parkinson's doctor appointment. Nothing new was reported. One morning I felt well enough to go with her into nearby Lambertville to try to sell a few antiques at one of this charming town's many shops. No luck there, but Carroll and I enjoyed a nice breakfast and good conversation about her father's and my health and our futures.

That weekend we all went to Ed and Wendy's for Wendy's retirement dinner. Many friends and family were there, including several of Alden's cousins. He was glad to be present but unable to participate. Neither was I. We left early. It would turn out to be his last family gathering.

I had set up the signing of our new wills and estate documents for a few days later. That was not to be. All was about to change suddenly and dramatically.

THREE

Death Without Warning

MY ONCOLOGY TEAM CONTINUED to dial back the doses I was given of the toxic chemicals intended to kill off any remaining cancer cells. But as the chemo dragged on, the harsh side effects of the drugs were taking an ever-greater toll on me and my capacity to cope. I felt weaker and sicker by the day, losing more hair, and barely able to manage my own daily needs, let alone those of Alden and Tyler at home and Tom at a distance. Carroll's rare visit was most welcome, as she helped out with meals, walking Tyler, and keeping her dad company. Her presence gave us both a lift, but especially Alden, who loved hearing about her family's adventures leading National Geographic expeditions in Mongolia, Bhutan, and Nepal. The week she arrived, in late September, was one of the most beautiful of the year in central New Jersey. Maybe both she, who spent much of her life outdoors, and her dad, who spent too much of his indoors, had cabin fever on September 24. Whatever compelled them to take their tennis racquets and head to the neighborhood courts that afternoon, it set in motion a chain of events that was to end tragically.

That date was a red-letter day in more than one way. The main event on all the national news was Pope Francis's unprecedented address that morning to both houses of Congress in Washington, DC. It was a stunningly impressive speech, calling our leadership to focus on the common good, compassion for the poor and disenfranchised, and the environmental integrity of the planet, our common home. As a Catholic Christian, I found it very moving that this humble, holy man, head of our church of 1.6 billion souls, brought such a powerful, prophetic message of justice, hope, and peace to world leaders.

By the time the Pope left to visit New York in mid-afternoon, my body's message was that it was time for a nap. That's when Carroll and Alden decided to go hit tennis balls. Remember that Alden suffered from a debilitating case of Parkinson's disease, a movement disorder. Even though he still visited a fitness center regularly and had participated in a movement program his PD doctor had prescribed, he couldn't move his feet quickly enough to get to a tennis ball coming across the net at him, however gently hit and slow-moving. And yet on this beautiful day during this very special visit from his daughter, he was going to try. I'm sure his intention as well as Carroll's was for him to stand in one spot while she hit balls directly to him so he could enjoy the aesthetics of the game and being outdoors on a sunny afternoon.

I was half asleep later when the phone rang. Carroll's low voice was on the other end. She was preparing me for something, taking her time getting to the point and hoping I wouldn't panic. It took a minute for me to get that her father had tripped and fallen on the court. Seeing his distress and inability to get up, she had called 911 for an ambulance to take him to the emergency room at the hospital near our home. They were there waiting to be seen by a doctor, who would admit Alden to the hospital. It dawned on me that the incident had happened more than an hour ago, and I was just hearing about it. Carroll tried to keep me calm, given my own condition, but there was no getting around it. X-rays showed that my husband had broken a large piece off his left hip bone. This was a man who had had not one, not two, but three hip replacements in the years I had known him. The third was a repair of the first. At his age a broken hip, given his condition and arthritic body, was most serious. Hanging up the phone, I felt anxiety rising within me and could hardly breathe. I started praying my go-to prayer for emergencies: "Lord, have mercy. Lord, have mercy." Numb with shock, I still had the presence of mind to put Tyler out for a few minutes, not knowing when I would be able to get home, then dressed and headed for the ER. I knew Alden's life and my own had changed dramatically, no matter what the outcome of this incident. All that preparation Ellen and I had done over the summer for what might happen if her father could not be maintained at home came to mind. Would he be long in the hospital, then rehab and a nursing home? He would hate that, I knew. But how could I manage his care given my own weakened condition?

These thoughts were set aside as I found my husband in the emergency room in great pain and distress. All that mattered was that he felt comforted and received good care. During the hours we spent with him that night, we tried to reassure him that his hip could heal—although we didn't know that—and that an orthopedic surgeon would view his X-rays and make recommendations.

We quickly learned that once in the hospital system you don't get to see your own doctors who know your conditions and might be able to contribute to the decisions about your treatment. Alden did not have access to either his primary care doctor or the orthopedist who had his medical history. Neither did I. Instead, the hospital relied on a relatively new category of doctor known as a "hospitalist," either an internist or family practice physician who specialized in hospital care. We later learned that the one in charge of Alden's case served several other hospitals as well and was stretched so thin that he complained to us that he didn't have adequate time for in-depth conversations about treatments because he had so many other patients! In retrospect, I should have complained to the hospital administrator. My husband remained in severe pain, waiting for an orthopedist of the hospital's choosing, who, like the hospitalist, was stretched across service to four or five local medical centers and didn't have time to get to him until mid-day the following day. Instead of good care, my husband was getting no care, at least from physicians. It took time for this to register with me, and after several exhausting hours I left Alden, who was lightly sleeping, in Carroll's hands.

The next day went from bad to worse. I remember sitting next to Alden in his room, watching on the overhead TV as Pope Francis arrived in Philadelphia for another major address. We were trying to focus on this world-shaping event while waiting for word from an orthopedic surgeon who had reviewed Alden's X-rays. It was nearly lunchtime before the hospital's doctor arrived. By this time I was not only anxious but mad. Why was my husband not seen much sooner? Why didn't we have a treatment plan for him after nearly eighteen hours in the hospital and him in great pain? This same doctor's only excuse was that he and the orthopedist hadn't had time to consult and were on call for several other hospitals. I told him in no uncertain terms at that point that I didn't care how thinly they were stretched. My husband was suffering and should have been treated hours ago, last night, in fact. Things were not going well.

After the orthopedic consult finally took place, the hospitalist reported that they had ruled out surgery to repair the hip, given Alden's age and condition. Instead, they had contacted a company that made braces to stabilize this kind of injury to send a representative to fit him for a brace. He would then spend several weeks in the brace, probably in a rehab facility, while the hip healed. This course of treatment was not going down well with any of us, but what choice was there? They believed Alden would not survive surgery and had nothing else to offer. The representative came soon afterward with several different braces, put Alden through agony while trying to fit him into one, then left. Alden was in so much pain that he could hardly stand it. By the time the physical therapist who came in later that day was through trying to make him stand in the ill-fitting, chafing brace, the poor man was done. His eyes rolled back in his head, his breathing was labored, and the nurse who came when we called down the hall for help called Code Blue. Alden had crashed. Carroll and I weren't allowed to stay with him but were herded out into the hall while the crash cart team gave him CPR and pounded on his chest, trying to revive him. Carroll and I held hands and prayed. How do you pray for a man you love who is going through such an ordeal? I can't remember my words, but I do know that I was asking God to relieve his pain, even if it meant he didn't come back. I knew he didn't want to go through prolonged, painful rehab and continuing decline from his Parkinson's. Maybe he was telling us—maybe God was telling us—that he'd had more than enough to handle this time, and it would be a blessing to be allowed to let go. Maybe, for him, this was his way out, through death to new life with God.

But he wasn't allowed to let go. Not then. The team resuscitated him, although they probably cracked at least one of his ribs in the process. He couldn't breathe normally after that. He was extremely agitated and yelled for those working on him to get away from him and take all the monitors and tubes off his body. They seemed to be putting him through unnecessary tests, hooking him up to heart monitors, breathing apparatus, one machine after another. I had never seen him so distressed. After the crash, he was moved into ICU, where he probably should have been all along, given his frailty and multiple conditions.

Carroll's brothers, Ed and Rob, came that afternoon, and were brought up to speed. I recall Alden saying to Ed that he was dying, and Ed responding that no, he wasn't. "You're not dying, Dad", he said, as you'd say to a child who was overreacting. Later, these words would haunt him. I had a flashback to a time when I was thirty-two years old and in a similar hospital room with my father, who said exactly the same thing to me. "I'm dying, Laura," he gasped, as his lungs full of emphysema were collapsing and the leukemia was killing the last of his red blood cells. "No, you're not, Dad," I'd said. "You'll come through this." We say these things not so much for them as for ourselves, out of our own anxiety and denial. My father was twenty years younger than Alden was at this time, but he was definitely dying. I left his room later that night without telling him how much I loved him and what he had meant to me and our family. I didn't have another chance. He died later that night.

Ed didn't mean to dismiss his father's awareness of his impending death. He just wasn't ready to believe it himself. None of us were. Alden's agitation continued. We all sat with him, trying to soothe and reassure him. Meanwhile, the Pope's visit continued to dominate the TV station in the room, although we watched with blank eyes. It felt surreal that the head of the Catholic Church should be in the same room with my dying husband and not help him. I wanted to yell at Pope Francis to get his attention, plead with him to pray for Alden, for whatever was for this dear, suffering man's highest good. At least let him be out of pain for a while and able to sleep, I begged. But the Pope's attention was elsewhere, and meanwhile my husband's life was ebbing away. Alden wasn't able to eat even simple hospital food like Jell-O and soup. He could sip iced tea or water, but at some level he was already beyond us. Did he have what we know as a near-death experience during those moments after he crashed? Did he reluctantly come back into his body? In his stress and anguish, he wasn't able to say.

The experience of the Code Blue and the crash cart team pounding on his chest that afternoon was another of those surreal experiences engraved in my memory. The sights and sounds of it, the anxiety and fear, the presences of hospital personnel rushing back and forth. A kind nurse trying to comfort me. Someone asked me if Alden had a DNR (Do Not Resuscitate) order. I knew he did and said so, but none of us was ready to invoke it at that point. After all, he had come into the hospital with just a broken hip, or a piece of a broken hip, not something life-threatening. Or so we thought.

We all waited hours to see if he would become less agitated. He did receive pain meds and at last, around 10 PM, was able to sleep fitfully. I thought it was safe to go home. His sons decided to stay with him a while longer. At some point that day had I gone home to let Tyler out and feed him? I couldn't remember for sure. I was done in myself and needed to try to rest. But that was not to be.

At 2:30 in the morning the phone rang. I was groggy but became alert. A nurse said she was concerned that Alden's blood pressure was low. They were pumping fluids into him, but he couldn't pass urine. It sounded as though his systems were shutting down. She also indicated that two different doctors had come in and had given what may have been conflicting orders. I asked if I needed to come in right then. In retrospect, I should have. At 3:15 the phone rang again. Alden was coding. I jumped out of bed, called Carroll, and we both got to the hospital at the same time to find the crash team pounding on his chest again. They had been at it for at least fifteen minutes. We knew he was gone. With a cry of anguish I told them to stop pounding on him. It was barbaric, I said. He'd had enough. "Let him go," I begged them. "Let him go." And they did. And he was gone, just like that, gone on a journey where I couldn't follow. There would be no postcards showing what he'd seen and saying "Wish you were here!," no phone messages with his familiar voice saying he was fine and would see me soon. I would not be able to share this final journey with him or hear back from him what it had been like. At least I thought so then.

After only thirty-six hours in the hospital, my husband, who had gone out to play tennis one beautiful fall afternoon with his visiting daughter, was dead. How could this be? I couldn't take it in. Carroll and I moved to either side of his body in his hospital bed. He didn't look peaceful. He looked as though he had died in agony. And I hadn't been there. I hadn't said goodbye when I left the night before in the way I would have if I had known he wouldn't be alive when I next saw him. I did tell him I loved him and would be back soon. So had his kids. But it was now too late to say any of those other things we wish we had said, just as it had been with my father forty years earlier.

We kissed his beloved face, now gray and devoid of life. I lifted his hand to take it in mine, but it felt cold and rubbery, and I dropped it. It felt like death. Carroll had to remove his wedding ring for me, as I couldn't do it once life had left his body. That wedding ring . . . it matched the gold band like mine that I had given him when we exchanged our wedding vows over twenty-six years earlier. He had lost the original while gardening a few years ago. Even renting a metal detector hadn't turned it up. Just before Christmas last year I had gone into Nassau Jewelers in downtown Princeton where we had purchased our original rings and ordered him a replacement just like the one he'd lost and had it similarly engraved. It came as a total surprise to him at Christmas, and he was very touched. That was the year of our twenty-fifth anniversary. He knew he was loved, and I knew I was—not only loved but deeply appreciated for who each of us was. While the last few years had been hard on both of us first because of his decline, then mine, the love remained intact, but different. It wasn't something I could reflect on then, only later.

The rest of the family was called. Ed, Wendy, and Rob got there as soon as they could. When I saw them, I told them, "He's gone." Just like that. He was gone. The him-ness of Alden, his particular being loved by all of us had moved on to a different and—we all at least hoped and most of us believed—a better place. Only the ravaged, yet beloved body remained. The five of us sat there in his room for over an hour, in shock, numb, trying to take it in, trying to figure out what had happened to cause his death and decide what to do next. Ed suggested a local mortuary service we could call to pick up the body. I knew Alden wanted to be cremated and so agreed. The rest of the arrangements would have to wait until I could think it through. Ironically, the day before had been the day we were scheduled to sign our updated wills with the estate planning attorney. It didn't change anything from the perspective of Alden's estate, but it did change what would now happen to mine. I couldn't think about that right then.

Later that day the hospitalist doctor called to say that Alden had died of a massive heart attack. How was that even possible, I wondered, given that he'd had a strong heart, no history of any cardiac issue. I was convinced then and remain convinced that Alden did not die from a heart attack. He died from poor hospital care and the overwhelming stress to his body dealt to him in very concentrated doses over that thirty-six–hour period. The other family members agreed with me. But what can you do about it? I wasn't going to sue, and his body was being cremated the next day. I wouldn't subject it to an autopsy. Death by what? Lack of coordinated care, of timely treatment, of mishandling of the case of an aged man with a complex disease? When you read obituaries of people who had Parkinson's disease, the obit never says that the person died of Parkinson's, but rather from complications of Parkinson's. How did a large chip of bone off a hip cause this man's death? I still don't know.

What I do know—and did then—is that my husband was out of pain. He was no longer suffering or distressed or afraid for his future. He was free of his ravaged body. He had, as my Benedictine sisters would say, gone home to God. That day, September 26, became Alden's Feast Day, the day of his passing from death into life after death, his entering into eternal life in the realms of light with God. But I was not yet ready to celebrate that. I was still taking in that he was gone, that I would go home to a house where his presence would still be felt in every room but from which he was paradoxically absent. Tyler would wonder where "Daddy" was and would miss him. People would call to talk with Alden, but he would be unable to come to the phone.

It was after 5 AM when I walked into that house now devoid of Alden's life force. Sleep was impossible, so I sat and waited until it was an hour at which I could make phone calls to let those closest to us know what had happened. Not knowing what else to do at this point, I also sent out email announcements and posted for my friends on Facebook that my husband had passed away. I just couldn't let more time pass before letting people know. They needed to know, I thought, that he had passed away, so they could start thinking of him as in another realm rather than as alive, here, waiting for their visit or call or invitation to go to breakfast. Assigning myself a task I could do almost mechanically helped me keep my mind off the trauma of death and the manner of his passing. And then the responses started coming in. I wasn't really ready for those yet, all the comments about how he would be missed and what a great man he had been. Later I would welcome that. Not now.

In the afternoon Rob, his wife Cat, and our grandson A.J., then eighteen, came for a welcome visit. Rob had been with his father through some of his ordeal and could relate to what I was feeling. Then Kate, our oldest granddaughter who lived nearby, came over with her husband, Matt, and their baby, Max. It was strange to have them visit without Alden's being there, I thought. He would have been so glad to see them. Louise, Alden's first wife and his children's mother, came by. We hugged, but couldn't speak of the deep loss we felt. Again, that sense of the surreal dominated the day. Normal things were going on, but nothing was normal anymore, and I had no idea what the new normal would look like. That evening Ellen flew in from Atlanta and stayed with me so I wouldn't be alone in the house. She had to sleep in Alden's bed, in his room. That felt very strange to both of us. Tyler couldn't figure out what was going on either and stuck to me like glue.

The family gathered the rest of that day and the next, as families do after a death, going through pictures, sharing memories, and making plans for Alden's funeral service the following Saturday. The Lutheran pastor of the church to which he belonged was notified and, thankfully, was available to conduct the service. The question of where Alden's ashes would go was settled by my choice: he would be interred in the new columbarium at that church, where Ed, Wendy, Kate, Matt, and Kate's sister Liz all worshipped. It was in a lovely, peaceful garden where they could sit and visit with him. The Dunham family plot in Green-Wood Cemetery in Brooklyn held generations of Alden's ancestors, but it was too distant from where he'd left his heart: with us here where we made our home.

On Sunday, the day after Alden's passing, Carroll came by to take me to Mass. I appreciated that my Buddhist stepdaughter stayed with me through the service. When the priest included Alden in the prayers for the dead, I lost it and cried through the rest of the Mass. Alden really was gone but was now remembered as one of the faithful who had gone home to the Lord. It was both shattering and yet comforting to hear his name called out as one whose soul was now in that intermediate state between death and the fullness of the afterlife who could be prayed for, that he might be fully united with God. That day I began to wonder about the nature of the afterlife and especially about purgatory, which the Catholic Church taught was a state of purification of the soul through which nearly all the dead passed before entering into God's glory in heaven. Later, this was to become the subject of much study and questioning on my part, and my conclusions will be shared in the chapter on the afterlife. At that time, I was still trying to come to terms with the fact that he had died and was not ready to wonder where he was. I trusted that he was in the merciful and loving presence of God. That was enough.

After Mass, while I longed to go home, rest, and be alone with my feelings, Carroll and I had to go to the funeral home to identify the body and do the paperwork for the cremation and the death certificates. It is just brutal for those newly widowed and bereaved to go through such a process, yet it must be done. I was thankful I didn't have to do it alone. When we walked in and were greeted by the staff person on duty, I could see in the room just off the entry Alden's dead body wrapped up to the chin in a sheet on a gurney. I was unprepared for this and shuddered and looked away. It was just too much. I had been thinking of him as gone, yet there he was, at least his beloved body. All of us react differently to seeing our loved ones when they have died. Open caskets used to be common in my youth, except when the bodies had been too disfigured, like my sister's, when she had died in a car accident at sixteen. Now, closed caskets are the norm when people are buried, but cremation is much more common, and we lose sight of the physicality of death when the loved one is not visible, as if not present.

Seeing my beloved like that with the mask of death on his face was unnerving. His mouth, open when he died, had been closed, and Carroll felt that he looked peaceful. When I came close and looked, I just thought he looked absent. I couldn't touch him at that point. I confessed earlier that I am a squeamish person, and this encounter with the physical dead body of the man I had loved for so many years was too much. To me, he wasn't there, not in that broken, bruised body, but somewhere in the realms of light, living still. That's what I clung to, as Carroll and I sat down in the conference room to handle the final disposition of Alden's body and grant his desire to be returned to ashes and dust.

In the meantime, the close family gathered at our—now my—house. They were going through boxes of pictures and papers to glean the best representations of Alden's life to be displayed at the reception after the funeral. I had very little to do with this process and was glad they had taken it over. It was much too soon for me to go through these boxes of memories.

Then it was time to meet with Dan, the Lutheran pastor who would conduct Alden's service. Having done dozens of funeral services myself during my years in the pastorate, I knew what was called for. I told Dan I would email him the Scriptures and hymns I preferred and that the family would talk about who would do what. Dan led us out behind the church to the garden and columbarium where Alden's ashes would rest. When I saw the niche where his urn would be placed, I broke down again. It was so final. And yet it was a lovely, simple, quiet, and peaceful place where family could gather now and then to pray and remember him and his love for us and ours for him.

We went to Ed and Wendy's then, where the family gathered for dinner. While it was being prepared, I sat quietly in the family room and watched the Pope's last Mass in Philadelphia. It was a fitting end to the Pontifical visit. His consecration of the body and blood of Christ in the great Eucharist celebration of God's enduring love for us and Christ's continuing presence in the bread and wine wrapped this weekend of death for me with a message of hope, love, and the promise of the resurrection of the dead for all the world's children of God.

Alden's obituary was a subject of discussion at dinner. Both Ellen and Ed agreed to do drafts, which I would then edit. Rob would get the final product into the local papers the next day. An obituary is a production. It summarizes the highlights of a person's life, his or her achievements, and the legacy he or she was leaving behind. Alden had had a distinguished career as a naval officer during the Korean War, later as Dean of Admissions at Princeton University, and finally as an influential grant-maker at the Carnegie Corporation of New York. The children naturally wanted as much as possible said about their dad, of whom they were justifiably proud. And Alden surely would have wanted us to mention his legacy of 50,000 trees he had planted at the old dairy farm in Pennsylvania that we all had loved. In addition to his degrees from Princeton, Harvard, and Columbia, should we mention his honorary degree from the University of California system? His prize-winning but obscure book, *Colleges of the Forgotten Americans*? His influence on higher education? What about his devotion to tennis? Also, we needed to be sure all the family members' spouses and children were included. The obituary began to grow.

What I found out that next day is that obits are very costly, and the last expenses, with the cremation, the obituaries, the funeral and reception, the urn and columbarium, began to add up alarmingly. I hadn't wanted to consider costs and didn't, really, yet they were part of what I had to deal with in the aftermath of my husband's sudden death. The financials and the loss of income resulting from his passing would take some time to sort out, and I definitely did not want to think about them at this point. This subject was something I pushed to the back burner until I was ready to—or at least had to—deal with it.

Finally, after a long, exhausting day, I was dropped off at home. Tyler was frantic for food, relief, and attention. I took care of him, then collapsed and went to bed. But I couldn't sleep for long. I lay awake from about 2:30 AM until I got up the next morning at around 5. It wasn't enough that I had lost my husband over the weekend; now, on Monday morning, I was being picked up at 9 AM to be taken to Fox Chase for my next chemo infusion. Yes, I could have cancelled it, but no, I didn't. I just wanted the whole thing over with. And now it was getting closer to the end.

That day I was too numb and exhausted to feel. I just went through the motions and procedures I had learned from my previous seven treatments. But layering chemo on top of everything else that had gone on almost took me down for the count. My blood pressure soared to nearly 200 over 100, and the infusion was delayed until it came down a bit. It was scary not only to me but also the staff in the infusion room, who seemed shocked that I had come in for the treatment so soon after my husband's death. Thankfully, I made it through the treatment. Carroll picked me up and dropped me at home. Ellen had left that morning but would be back for the weekend. I still needed to edit the obituary and get it to Rob so that it could be placed in the newspapers in the next couple of days in time for people to hear about Alden's death and upcoming funeral. There was no time to feel or think about what was going on. Too much was happening, too much pressure to get things done that needed to be done in a timely manner, and my whole being was protesting all the way.

Later that day my dear friend and spiritual director, Theresa, called from St. Ben's Monastery in Minnesota. We had a good, long talk that lifted my spirits and helped me feel supported through this ordeal that, upon Alden's death, had entered into the worst period of my extraordinary time. There was no respite except for Theresa's call. The next one I received was the funeral home with the news that Alden had been cremated. His ashes would be delivered to me the next day. That was just too much for me to absorb. I couldn't think about his dear body now reduced to a few pounds of ashes. The rest of the day was a blur.

But the following day there was something I felt I urgently needed to do. I needed to get my new will signed. I made arrangements with the estate attorney to go to his office and do this to relieve my mind about what would happen to Tom if I died as suddenly as had Alden. The attorney reassured me that Alden's former will was just fine and that it didn't really matter that he hadn't gotten to sign his new one. We knew what his intentions were, and they would be carried out. I called Tom after I got home and told him that all was well with the estate plan and that my good friend Christine had agreed to be the trustee of a trust for him in the event I died before him. While he was still too distraught over Alden's passing and my situation to take this in, he did thank me and seemed somewhat relieved that a plan was in place to provide for his support. With a severe anxiety condition, Tom did not need to be worrying about losing me, too.

Ironically, I believed that I came close to death that day I signed my new will. When my daughter-in-law Wendy came over to disconnect the chemo canister I had been wearing since my last infusion, something went wrong. I think air bubbles got into the port in my chest during the disconnect. At any rate, after she left I was certain I was either going to pass out or die. Frantically, I called my doctor's office—no help—then Fox Chase. Thankfully, the oncology nurse and the doctor's associate talked me through the episode, and it eventually passed. However, I remained weak and shaky and sleep-deprived. Louise kindly came over and sat with me until I felt better and brought me chicken soup, truly for the soul.

This episode was the first in a series of incidents to trigger severe anxiety on my part. Over the next few months I would be certain on a number of occasions that I was going to have a heart attack or stroke or pass out. That I didn't I believe was only because of the grace of God.

The next day was filled with the family gathering again to finalize the funeral and reception arrangements, now one day away. I just wanted to get through it. Since most of my hair was gone because of the chemo, I planned to wear a black hat with my widow's black outfit and was grateful I had one so that I didn't have to try to buy something appropriate. Everyone would know what I had been going through, so I wasn't focused on trying to look anything more than presentable. It would be all I could do to put myself together and get through the day.

October 3, the day of Alden's memorial service, was cold, rainy, and windy. It seemed fitting that nature was reflecting my mood on this somber day. I know that I was being prayed for mightily. I could feel the energy of that. Emails and cards confirmed that friends were supporting me through this formal goodbye to my husband.

The whole Dunham family gathered at the church. All six grandchildren—Kate and Liz, Kacie and A.J., Liam and Galen, and the one great-grandchild, Max—had come from far and near, and all of them looked great. Alden would have been so proud of them. I'm sure he was present and seeing the whole panorama from his new perspective. Over a hundred friends and extended family attended also. The service was lovely. Kacie, then a sophomore at Vanderbilt University, sang the Twenty-Third Psalm in her beautiful soprano voice. Other family read Scripture and remembrances. Ed's eulogy for his father was very well done, and Alden would have enjoyed it as well as Pastor Dan's homily on Romans 8. St. Paul's beautiful, thrilling words resonated deeply within me: "For I am convinced that neither death, nor life, nor angels, nor rulers, nor things present, nor things to come, nor powers, nor height, nor depth, nor anything else in all creation, will be able to separate us from the love of God in Christ Jesus our Lord."[1] I wept quietly and knew it was so.

Afterwards, Dan led us into the columbarium for the interment. Liam, the oldest grandson, placed his grandfather's ashes in the niche where they would rest. This touched me deeply, and I couldn't stop crying as the niche door was closed, and I saw Alden's name with his birth and death dates

---

1. Rom 8:38–39.

engraved on the front. It all seemed so final at that point, truly the closing of a door on a long life and on our marriage.

The luncheon reception was held at the church. We greeted friends and extended family throughout the afternoon. The Dunham children and grandchildren led those gathered through the highlights of Alden's life using a slideshow and photo boards set up on a long table. There was enough laughter to balance the tears. Tom was represented through a lovely, funny reflection he had written about his stepfather. The grands led a rousing rendition of the song their grandfather always sang to them when they appeared in the morning: "Good morning, Breakfast Clubbers." No one can sing it quite as off-key as their grandfather, however. After all the guests had left, the family gathered for a time at Ed and Wendy's. No one wanted to leave, as it was likely the last time all would be together until another such occasion. I had touching conversations with several of the grandchildren, then was too exhausted to stay on. That night, with the funeral, reception, and family gathering behind me, I could at last sleep for a few hours.

I was able to attend Mass the next morning before the family came over to our house for omelets, the specialty of Ellen's husband, Phil. It was time to begin to pass on some of Alden's belongings to whomever wanted them. This was the beginning of that process, which went on for several weeks, then months, before it was time to leave our home for good. That afternoon, I took Ellen and Phil to the small nearby airport for their flight back to Atlanta and came home to an empty house. After all the activity of the past ten days since Alden's accident, I felt especially alone, anxious, and afraid. I was thankful for the dear company of my faithful companion, Tyler, Prince of Dogs.

I didn't have time to grieve, not then, and not for a long while. When Monday came, I had the Ignatian group to attend to on their bi-weekly call, a scheduled meeting at my church, and several other stops to make. On my list were also all the notifications to be done in the event of a death: Social Security, the pension company, investment firms, banks, and so on. Fortunately, since I had been a Certified Financial Planner for many years, even after I went into the ministry, I had the capacity to deal with all these financial details. What I didn't have was the desire or the energy. Yet these things had to be done, and there was no one else to do them. When I ran a financial planning firm for several years in Princeton many years before, I had often dealt with clients who were widows in similar circumstances to those in which I now found myself. Many of them had never handled their own finances, the carry-over from an era when such things weren't expected of married women. Educating them and helping them to find good advisors was part of my role, but I knew how overwhelming it could be to those newly widowed and without the emotional resources to deal with all that was required of them.

That afternoon Carroll and Louise came by for tea and to take Tyler for a walk. I was grateful for their company. Steve from the funeral home stopped over to deliver the death certificates needed to change over the financial records. After a couple of days mostly on my own, it was good to have people stopping by who had shared the experience of losing Alden.

Later that day, something significant happened to me for the first time. I felt my husband's energy around me, a strong presence and somewhat chaotic. Because of the energy healing work I had done for years, I knew what was going on. Sadly, I had to ask him to stay at a bit of a distance, because the erratic nature of his energy at that point was elevating my blood pressure and heart rate. I told him I loved and missed him and was glad he had come to tell me he was all right. I believe that after people have crossed through death, they learn in the afterlife how to connect from time to time with our denser human energy and to make contact with loved ones. More will be said of this later. For now, I was just glad to know Alden was able to be present to me. Free of his body and existing in consciousness and spirit, my husband's death was now over, and he was experiencing his new life in a higher dimension. I was happy for him but at the same time was moving into a new, troubling phase in my own life as a widow and cancer patient whose condition continued to deteriorate.

What my life would be like in the near future now became my focus, as it was clear to me that I could no longer afford both to maintain the home I was in and support Tom's living expenses in California. While the conventional wisdom for new widows is to take at least a year to make a major decision, especially if it involves a change of housing or a long-distance move, I couldn't wait that long. My extraordinary time was morphing into a whole new phase, that of major transition. And at that point it wasn't going well.

FOUR

Transition: Stranger in a Strange Land

WHILE I BEGAN TO adjust to my new state, life went on around me. Family members were getting back into their daily routines, but I no longer had one. What I dealt with every day now were increasingly serious side effects from the chemo and trauma to my body and emotions. I was starting to fear what each day would bring.

Less than two weeks after Alden's passing I began to have swallowing problems. At first it felt as though something was caught in my throat and wouldn't go down. It might take four hours for a small pill to pass through my esophagus, and larger ones had to be pulverized or dissolved in liquid. Then I began to have what I called "episodes." These consisted of waking up in the middle of the night shaking or having a body flush reaction to some food I was trying to swallow. One episode happened while I was having breakfast at the neighborhood diner with Christine. I started to choke and thought I would pass out. Christine got me into her car and rushed me to my doctor's office. Thankfully, he was able to see me. He thought the problem might be acid reflux and put me on a liquid form of antacid, a med I continued to take for over a year. And yet that wasn't the cause of the problem, as I continued to experience these episodes for some time. They produced considerable anxiety, as you can imagine, especially since I was alone in my home when most of them happened.

Not long after this first episode, another bout with shaking and choking led me to the emergency room at the hospital where Alden had died. Being there probably exacerbated the severity of the episode, and I waited anxiously for several hours while the medical staff tried to figure out what was going on. They couldn't come up with anything, gave me Benadryl in case I was allergic to something I ate (go figure), and sent me home. The next day my oncologist wanted to see me in Fox Chase's urgent care facility, so that week was taken up with medical emergency appointments with no resulting diagnoses of my mysterious maladies.

The oncologist then scheduled me for an endoscopy, a procedure kind of like a colonoscopy, except from the other end. A lighted tube goes down your throat and examines it for blockages or abnormalities. I made it through that one okay, but continued to have swallowing problems so that for a period that lasted about two months I couldn't eat anything that wasn't pureed. Once I heated up a frozen pot pie for dinner, then threw it into my VitaMix, which can macerate just about anything. What came out looked and tasted like brown glue. Needless to say, during this period I lost weight. My oncologists weren't happy about that, although I thought it was the one beneficial effect of chemo I had experienced so far. Later on another swallowing test was done involving barium with X-rays read by a speech therapist. I found that puzzling, but the therapist was there to observe how I was swallowing. Who knew they did such things? Even she couldn't come up with any possible explanation for the problem other than a "motility issue" in a muscle in the back of my throat. It didn't seem to any of us a reason for what was occurring. Another mystery. Metaphorically, did the swallowing issue mean I was fed up or couldn't swallow all the awful things that were happening to me? I still don't know.

That Thanksgiving, I wasn't able to participate in the family dinner, two months after Alden's death. Pureed turkey isn't a pretty picture, and I had lost my appetite for just about all food during this time anyway, subsisting on fresh soups and protein shakes. I also realized that I wasn't very good company at festive occasions and didn't want to impose my sad self on others. In retrospect, this wasn't a good decision, but then I wasn't making many good ones at that time.

One of the most distressing consequences of my inability to swallow was how it limited my participation in Mass. Not only was I unable to sing the liturgical responses and hymns, but I couldn't swallow the consecrated Host, the body of Christ, without drinking at least half a bottle of water afterward. I did not share the common cup of wine, the blood of Christ, because I had so many toxins in my body that I didn't want to pass them on, nor, with a compromised immune system, to receive other people's germs and viruses. I realized even then that this was symptomatic of my anxiety and not consistent with our Catholic belief in the nature of transubstantiation of the body and blood. Despite these limitations, when it came down to the essence of participation in the worship of God, receiving the sacrament of the Eucharist, I was able to consume the communion bread or wafer, and that was a gracious plenty.

In addition to my eating and swallowing problems, my blood pressure continued to alarm my medical team. I had to purchase a BP cuff from the pharmacy, take my pressure twice a day, and record the results. My primary care doctor put me on a blood pressure medicine, so now I was on several new meds that also had side effects, in addition to those caused by the chemo.

Worse than the physical symptoms, which I thought might go away after the chemo worked its way out of my body, was the anxiety condition that developed in the wake of all my stress. Since my son has suffered from this condition for years, I had seen its devastating effects up close. He still takes medication daily to keep it in check. It takes very little to trigger a panic attack in him, which causes heart palpitations, heat and chills, shortness of breath, and dizziness, just to mention the physical symptoms.

Such attacks began to happen in me, mostly triggered by my fear that I would choke to death while alone in the house, or by almost anything else that would create a sense of vulnerability or abnormal stress. I felt out of control of my body and life circumstances, which indeed I was. One day I was just sitting in bed, watching repeats of those Hallmark Channel Christmas movies that start in October, when I experienced what felt to me like a heart attack. Since there was no way I was going to return to the ER at the local hospital, I called Christine in a panic. She came right away to sit with me and, given her own experience with panic attacks in family members, explained that she thought that was what I was having. My doctor had prescribed some medication, which I was reluctant to take because of all the other meds and side effects, but after taking one I did feel better. Now I began to take a small dose daily to try to keep the anxiety in check.

During this time I went to another hospital where the wonderful Sr. Pat offered energy healing work with prayer. I had seen her several times and always looked forward to these sessions, which helped rebalance my energy fields and left me feeling calm and peaceful. On this occasion, as Sr. Pat met me in the waiting area to escort me to the healing room, I started to feel very dizzy and faint. I had to sit down and take my anxiety medication. Meanwhile, a nurse came by and took my BP, which was an alarming 200 over 100. She wanted me to go to this hospital's ER. Oh, no, I thought. I just couldn't go through another emergency room experience. Sr. Pat called in the family friend who manages the healing center in the hospital, who stayed with me for some time, and then, at my request, drove me home. I decided I'd rather expire at home than in another cold, sterile emergency room. And I did feel better when I got home.

As you might imagine, this string of episodes with no apparent cause left me feeling anxious and vulnerable. I spent more and more time at home alone, just sitting in the club chair in my study/prayer room listening to sacred music. The elevated vibration of chant and polyphony was music to my heart as well as my ears, and it played a soothing role in my eventual recovery. I had purchased a forty-CD set called *Sacred Music* that spanned late antiquity through the twentieth century. My practice became to sit in silence each day listening to one of these CDs for about an hour and continue with contemplative, silent prayer, resting in the presence of God. This for me was healing, at least at the level of the emotions and the spirit.

Christine was a constant presence during this traumatic time. We worked out a system of staying in touch so that I wouldn't fear dying alone and no one finding my decomposing body for days or taking care of my dear Tyler. Despite years of spiritual practice, such as daily *Lectio Divina* and Ignatian imaginative prayer, both usually deeply contemplative and calming, my anxious thoughts would not go away. I would imagine myself choking to death or having a stroke or being unable to breathe, and Tom and Tyler being left to fend for themselves. These weren't totally irrational thoughts, just exaggerations of possible outcomes given my condition and circumstances. To relieve my anxiety, I would text Christine each morning to let her know I was still around. If she didn't hear from me by 8 AM she would call. If no answer, she would call my daughter-in-law Wendy, who lived nearby, to go check on me. This system offered me reassurance and relief from my acute fear of dying without anyone knowing. Habits die hard, and Christine and I still text each morning to this day, although we now live 2,700 miles apart. I am eternally grateful to this dear woman who holds a prominent place among my Communion of Saints.

Even while all these episodes and conditions were occurring, I stayed hopeful that at least some of them would be temporary and that after I stopped chemotherapy they would begin to go away. I was scheduled for my ninth infusion on October 12, a day I remember well, because it turned out to be the final treatment. Both my oncology team and I decided, given all that was going on, to stop the protocol. So I managed to complete only nine of twelve prescribed treatments. Would they be enough to kill off all the cancer and prevent it from coming back, at least for a time? My doctors seemed to think so, and I certainly had had enough. I couldn't imagine that any errant cancer cells had managed to escape what was ravaging my body. What a relief not to have to face those last three treatments!

I continued to see my doctors at Fox Chase regularly for checkups for the next few months. CT scans are called for every three months in the first year or so after finishing chemo, and I went through a couple of those in October and February. Anyone who's had one knows how unpleasant that process is, but by now I was a veteran of uncomfortable hospital tests. Except for causing hematomas in my hands, where the large needles went in to insert the dye in my veins, I got through the scans okay. And the results showed no presence of cancer, thanks be to God.

Despite all of this trauma and anxiety, I continued trying to keep up with guiding the group of five women through the Ignatian Exercises. They were now preparing for their final retreat. And, believe it or not, I had committed to present a full-day retreat and a four-week class on "Advent with Mary" at my parish. "What was I thinking?," you well might ask. This is the work I love to do, so I was happy to be engaged in it. Being able to work with this sacred, nourishing material felt like a sanity break from all the medical stuff going on. Yet it required a huge effort on my part not only to prepare for these events but to be fully present and at my best to lead them.

After nearly eight months, the dedicated women completing the Exercises were ready to make their final commitment to God and to following Jesus Christ by praying the "Take and receive" prayer of St. Ignatius. To pray the *Suscipe* sincerely is a huge commitment, one none of us took lightly. I had made this commitment myself several years earlier, and now was a particularly good time to renew it. In these past months I had had to surrender my life to God not just in words but through complete, abject submission of body, heart, mind, and soul. Control had been taken out of my hands, and I was left an anxious mess. I had prayed that prayer enough times over the past few years to believe I meant it, but experiencing the effects of turning over my complete self to God was something else. Sometimes it felt like a test of whether I really understood what I prayed.

Later I will share the experiences of more saintly women and men who reached this point of total surrender to whatever was God's desire for their lives. I have learned much from them about suffering and enduring. My years as a Benedictine oblate had exposed me to the monastic life, especially as lived by the women of St. Benedict's Monastery in Minnesota, where I was affiliated. All of them made vows which included a version of the *Suscipe* prayer, asking God and their community to take and receive their whole selves just as they were and support them in living the monastic life to which God had led them and which they fully chose. As an oblate, I had for some years tried to live in accordance with the Rule of Benedict outside the monastery and to discern God's desires for me. Now I had to lay aside my striving and simply let go, free-falling into the safety and protection of God's love. No other way would take me through this traumatic time.

In November the Ignatian group gathered at the home of one of the women for a half-day retreat to conclude the Exercises. I was proud of each of them for the perseverance shown during these many demanding months. I was also grateful for the concern and support they had shown me during this time. Their deep reflections and sharing of their insights and experiences over the course of walking with Jesus through his ministry, his passion, and his resurrection and ascension were testimony to their deepened faith and spiritual growth. We had a wonderful day together and parted friends, prepared to stay in touch. We did more than that over the next year, deciding to study and reflect together on several of the church's luminous, exceptional mystics, like St. Hildegard of Bingen and Julian of Norwich. Such deep, small group work is so nourishing spiritually and builds up the body of Christ so effectively that my prayer is for all people of faith to have such opportunities to study and pray together. Most such groups are self-forming, rather than initiated by the churches, unless during the seasons of Advent and Lent, when most such activity takes place. During this time of significant change and transition for me, being with this special group of women was like taking a mental health break. While I was relieved to have been able to have the stamina to see them through the Exercises in which they engaged so remarkably well, I also knew I would miss our bi-weekly calls and their loving presence in my life on a regular basis.

And suddenly it was Advent, my favorite time of year, the four-plus weeks leading up to Christmas. I love the sense of deep stillness while waiting in anticipation of the fulfillment of the Old Testament prophecies of the coming of the Messiah. I especially love the Annunciation of the Archangel Gabriel to Mary and the Visitation of Mary to her kinswoman Elizabeth, mother of the prophet John the Baptist, who would point the way to Christ as the Son of God. When I felt well enough, I prepared for the retreat and classes by constructing an extensive PowerPoint presentation drawing on Scripture, art, music, and poetry from the sequence of movements which take place during this liturgical season of Advent and Christmastide: the Annunciation, the Visitation, the Nativity, and the Adoration of the Magi, followed by the Flight into Egypt. I looked forward to the presentations, although the preparation was exhausting and had to be done during those few hours each day when I was feeling able to work.

During these months of November and December, despite and because of all that was going on, it became clear to me that I was going to have to put my house on the market after the first of the year and move to live with my son. The prospect of a long-distance move and what it would entail while in my condition was more than daunting. I thought often about St. Paul's admonition that God wouldn't give us more than we could endure, and that a way out would be provided. Alden's way out had been death, but I wasn't ready to go yet, not while Tom needed my presence and support to help improve his quality of life and deal with his health issues. And so I began to prepare for the move by finishing cleaning out Alden's bedroom and bath, passing on to the family what they would like to have and giving most of the rest away. That Christmas I would gift only items that weren't going to make the move with me, and there was a considerable amount of stuff that qualified. As I sorted through clothing, books, pictures, housewares, and furnishings, I thought of each family member and friend who would receive one of these gifts and set aside something I thought he or she would not only like but treasure.

Both Alden and I had valued books and had given away hundreds each time we had moved. What remained of his was a special collection on American education, especially higher education, which had been his professional field and his specialization in grant-making. He also had some literary classics in special editions. Together I thought these might appeal to the educated customers of an independent bookstore in Princeton, across the street from the university. I talked with the bookstore, secured their interest, and began to catalog and box up these books.

As it turned out, this activity led to another physical collapse. It seemed I hadn't yet reached the fullest level of surrender. Since there was no one around to help, I tried to lift full boxes of heavy books and carry them out to my car to transport to the bookstore. Not a wise decision. I started having severe back pain. One night it was so bad I could not even move from my bed to the bathroom. I have to say that this was probably the low point of this whole, never-ending ordeal. With my husband gone, alone in the house except for Tyler, and now incapable of moving without excruciating pain and back spasms, I cried out to God for mercy. After much agony from trying to inch my way to the phone beside my bed, I managed to call Wendy, who had been asleep and wasn't responsive to my fear and need for help. What was I to do? I lay there in the dark praying for my angels and guides to help me. Eventually I was able to slide off the bed and get to the bathroom, but the pain almost caused me to pass out. I lay awake most of the night and contacted Christine in the morning. She came by, took care of Tyler, and got my doctor on the phone. All he had to offer was Ibuprofen.

Although it was now the week before Christmas, I managed to get an appointment with an orthopedic back specialist. After X-rays, he pronounced that I had a compression fracture at L4, one of the lower vertebrae. The good news was that it would heal by itself. No surgery was required and no treatment until I was able to tolerate some physical therapy to strengthen my core muscles to keep the back supported. Pain continued, and I despaired of getting through the holidays without incident. I had already missed Thanksgiving with my swallowing problems; now it was likely I'd miss participating in Christmas as well. So be it, I thought. I wasn't up to going to all the family and friends' gatherings anyway. I would celebrate a quiet Christmas Eve and Christmas Day at home and be grateful for the gift of the Christ child.

It did work out that I was able to join the family on Christmas morning for the gift exchange and later in the day for a festive dinner, at which I was actually able to tolerate a little soft food. That was progress. Alden was much missed, and I kept interjecting memories of him or what he would have enjoyed about the day into the conversation to keep his presence in mind.

The back fracture led to an appointment with an endocrinologist, who after the first of the year did a bone density test to determine whether I had osteoporosis or the lesser condition of osteopenia. I was borderline between the two conditions, which meant I needed to do something to strengthen my bones or the kind of fracture I had experienced would happen again. The doctor recommended a strong medication that I declined, as one of its side effects could have been a broken jaw! I mean, really. You've probably seen the ads for it on TV. Who would take such powerful drugs after hearing the list of possible side effects? Because of my experience of having the worst form of every side effect of my chemo protocol, I was now overly sensitive to medications and had become a minimalist, taking only what was absolutely necessary. In fact, a few weeks earlier, when I went in for a routine flu shot, I almost passed out afterwards. I had the shakes, dizziness, and weakness, and had to wait in the doctor's office for over an hour until I felt okay to drive home. For several days afterwards, I suffered the after effects of that shot, the high dose one recommended for seniors vulnerable to the flu. I have not had a flu shot since. Just shows how skeptical I had become of conventional medicine and pharmaceutical solutions. My son, having lived in California for several years, had come to believe in the naturopathic way and was now a vegan. He too had suffered severe side effects from prescribed medicines and felt permanently harmed by them. I was beginning to see his point.

The year 2015 with all of its traumas and major changes finally came to an end. I spent a couple of hours at Christine's home on New Year's Eve with her, her husband, and another friend, giving thanks for having survived the ordeals of the year and praying for a better 2016.

Tom was disappointed that he would have to spend another Christmas by himself, but I told him I simply wasn't well enough to travel. We talked several times throughout the season and began to consider where we would live. Tom wanted to stay in California. That was just about the last place I wanted to live. After much discussion, consideration of other places, and prayerful discernment, I began to realize that for Tom's best interests and continuity, California made the most sense. But I ruled out the Los Angeles area, not only because of cost but also because it just didn't feel like a place where I could find the kind of community I needed to support my semi-monastic existence.

To move things along toward our deciding about a move, I booked my flight to LA the last week in January, the time of Tom's birthday. It would turn out to be a house-hunting trip, although that wasn't the main purpose at the time I arranged the travel. It was to find out how Tom was doing and set up better home health care for him. The new year would bring even more changes, and one of the most significant ones was about to be set in motion.

Life began to move even more quickly as we got past the holidays. I met with a realtor and agreed to put my home on the market in mid-February, thinking it might sell by the summer and that I would be resettled somewhere by the fall, about a year after Alden's death. On my January trip to California Tom and I did spend a couple of days with a realtor checking out a possible area in which to live. That place didn't seem workable for him, so we put on hold any further moving plans until my house in New Jersey should sell. We were able to spend some good time together, and he was much relieved about his own situation to know that I would soon be joining him.

When I returned home, I had to prepare the place for sale, so cleaning out and cleaning up continued, even with my back still painful and my heart disconsolate over the move. As Valentine's Day approached, my house was listed. Then—surprise! It went under contract in less than two weeks. This sped up my relocation timetable considerably, so the January trip to California, which had taken all my physical resources and drained my finances, was repeated a month later. By then it was clear that I needed to find a home for Tom and me, and, like it or not, it was going to be in Southern California. I had done some research and had settled on Riverside, a city of over 300,000 in what was known as the Inland Empire, about sixty miles east of Los Angeles. Tom felt that if he were ever to have a chance to participate in the music business—his lifelong dream—he needed access to LA. He also needed access to clinics and medical care that could be found in a large community like Riverside. Neither of us had ever been there before, but I flew out to LA again in late February to check it out. We now had the time pressure with the sale of the New Jersey house pending.

Tom and I met our realtor in Riverside to tour homes that might suit us. Mind you, an elderly contemplative living with her rock musician son, a large dog, and two cats was not an easy demographic to work with. We needed a single-family home where Tom could house his studio, I could have a bedroom and a study/prayer room away from the music space, and Tyler could have an enclosed yard. At the end of the first day of house-hunting, we had no contenders. We decided to stop at a restaurant for a bite before heading back to LA. Big mistake. The afternoon sun was so bright that when I walked into the place through its glass doors and turned left toward the ordering counter, I walked straight into a plate glass window I couldn't see. My head cracked against the thick glass and blood started to gush out. The whole experience was about as surreal as anything I had experienced during this extraordinary time. Needless to say, I refused the EMT's request to go to the hospital ER, given my phobia, and instead had Tom take me to a nearby urgent care facility. Hours later, with my forehead taped together and bandaged, Tom, who rarely drives at all, was assigned the task of getting us back to LA at night on the congested freeways. Thanks be to God, he managed it and became my hero as a result. I was never so glad to see a bed in a motel as that night.

We took the next day to rest before trekking again to Riverside to try to find a house. Not much was on the market in our price range, so it was easy to narrow down what was left to two contenders. By the end of the day, we had pretty well settled on our new home. As I was to return to New Jersey a day later, I waited until I returned home to make the offer. Fortunately, it was accepted, and we knew where we would be by late April. Despite my head injury and not knowing anything about our new community, we would have a place to call home. The house we were purchasing had an addition of a large bedroom-studio space for Tom downstairs, and the master suite upstairs, far enough away from his space to allow for privacy and at least a modicum of quiet. And it had a small but adequate yard for Tyler and was sufficiently updated so that I didn't need to spend more on renovations. That was a good thing, as the cost of the home was maxing my budget, and I couldn't begin to think about what it would cost to move me and my stuff across the country.

By the end of February, during Lent, I was thrust into the new drama of all the paperwork and processes required to sell one home and buy another. Even though Alden and I had renovated our home in New Jersey, there was much more to do, and the work required on the home after the inspection was both surprising and expensive. If you've ever had to install a Radon detection system, you'll know what I mean. But as the process unfolded, it seemed likely that by two weeks after Easter I would become a California resident. Meanwhile, I was supposed to be leading a retreat during Lent, which would also be presented as a four-week class, "Lent with the Mystics," which needed a great deal of my time and attention to prepare. "Lord, have mercy!" became my constant mantra. My health was still precarious, and I nearly fainted one afternoon while presenting the Mystics class. How I managed it all with people enthusiastic about the class is one of God's mysteries and miracles. My Communion of Saints pulled me through.

With all the inspections and negotiations going on at both houses, I still had a long list of things to get settled quickly in New Jersey. Going through all my stuff and deciding what to take and what to leave occupied my spare time and limited energy. I couldn't face the thought of having to furnish the house in Riverside as soon as I got there, so I decided to keep most of my furniture, even though it would be costly to move. I figured it would cost just as much in my stamina and cash to try to find and buy furnishings for the new house. As it turned out, that was a good decision, as everything fit and I only needed to find a small dining set for the new place. But one huge task remained: getting rid of what I couldn't take. That meant giving up many treasured belongings, like my twelve place settings of Santa Fe Railroad china, something I'd lugged around and loved for over a dozen years. It would not make the trip to California, I knew, because I would no longer be giving dinner parties or possibly even having guests for meals, now that I would be living with my son. It would just be too costly to pack and move all that china and the serving pieces. I would have to sell it, along with quite a bit more. That entailed hiring an estate sale person to set up, price, and sell as much as possible for me in April, just before I was to vacate the house. What that involved was much more than I had anticipated and resulted in much less money than I thought I would realize. I also ended up having to get rid of everything left over. That took forever to arrange in itself.

Moving isn't fun, and even though I had endured it many times, this time was the hardest of all because of the reason for the move and the facts that A) I didn't feel well; and B) I really didn't want to move to Southern California, a place where I knew no one but my son, who didn't know anyone there either. It felt as though I would literally become a stranger in a strange land. I already was a stranger in the strange land of widowhood and recovering from a dread disease and its aftermath.

Thinking about this move now, with a little hindsight, it sounds a bit irrational to have done it. Who moves across the country a few months after her husband dies, away from family and friends to a strange place she doesn't even want to go? That would be me. But I had sought to listen for and to understand God's desire in this, and it was clearly for Tom and me to join forces and support one another through whatever lay ahead. Confident of the outcome of this crucial discernment, I went about carrying out this transition of such magnitude with whatever strength, courage, and reason I could muster. Talk about surrendering your will. It was time for me to become less and Tom to become more. I thought about that in biblical terms. Just as John the Baptist had stepped aside in favor of his kinsman, Jesus, I felt that I'd pretty much fulfilled the purpose of my life, and it was time for Tom to fulfill his. But I don't think God saw it quite that way—not yet, anyway.

While Alden and I had lived in New Jersey for less than three years, we had lived there much longer previously, and leaving there meant leaving the resident Dunham family behind, along with a few good friends, like Christine, who'd gotten me through the past demented year, and my parish, where I was able to lead retreats, teach classes, and enjoy being part of the community. All that would come to an end with this move. With everything that was going on, I didn't have time to process my feelings about leaving. There was no time to grieve Alden's death, either, in the wake of my chemo and ongoing health issues.

Somehow, despite all the glitches that emerged in the process of selling the one house and buying the other, it all managed to come together. The hand of God, with the help of the Communion of Saints, had to have been at work to make it all happen. Finally, the moving van came and took what was making the journey to the West Coast. That night Tyler and I were truly alone in the empty house with the echoes of our life there with Alden, and it felt very sad and lonely. Tyler clung to me, totally confused by what was going on. We both were ready to leave this forlorn space. I had managed to get my doctor to designate Tyler as an emotional support animal, which entitled me to take him, big as he was, with me in the main cabin of the plane flying us nonstop from Philadelphia to LAX. Christine kindly agreed to accompany us and help us get through Tom's move from his apartment into the new house and to spend a few days overseeing our settling in in Riverside. So very early a couple of mornings later a limo service picked us up, and our journey to California began. Tyler did incredibly well, managing to make it through the long flight and the baggage claim on the other end and a while longer until I could take him outside the airport and find a nice green patch on which he could relieve himself. That simple but urgent act marked the beginning of our new life as strangers in a strange land.

Getting Tom packed up and ready to move the next day was another ordeal. Suffice it to say that if Christine hadn't been there I don't know how it could have been accomplished, as Tom had been able to do little to prepare on his own. Finally, the moving truck left his place, we turned in his keys to the rental office, and, with Tyler, Tom, and his two rescue cats, Sebastien and Emily, in the back seat of Tom's car, we began the two-hour drive to Riverside. Thankfully, the house closing and recording of deed had occurred in our absence earlier in the day, so we met Tom's van at the new house and moved his stuff in. Christine and I slept on air mattresses for the days until my van arrived from New Jersey, with most everything intact.

Now housed and together, the transition to our new life was launched. Next up was getting Tom's health insurance and ID cards transferred from Los Angeles County to Riverside County and setting him up in a new clinic. Sparing you the details, let me just say that it was all excruciating, time-consuming, and did not go well. Christine left, and we were alone with each other and our vastly changed circumstances. The beginning of life in Riverside near the end of April of 2016 marks the official end of that intense, emotional roller coast ride I have called my extraordinary time, although in some ways it remains just that.

Fast forward to over a year and a half later. As I write, we're completing Advent, 2017. The adjustments Tom and I have had to make both to living together and living here have been more challenging than either of us imagined, requiring us to accommodate each other's needs and feelings with flexibility, acceptance, and grace. Our relationship is much different from when we were decades younger. Then I was clearly the parent and he the child, and he had to play more or less by my rules. Now we're two adults with contrasting personalities, interests, and agendas sharing a home and trying to construct a mutually caring, respectful relationship with more reciprocity than ever before. If that doesn't sound easy, it hasn't been for either of us. But I have come to know my son's heart in a way I never would have were we not so much in each other's company, and he has come to know who I am other than his mother. In a way, we are each other's mirrors, holding up what the other needs to see about him- or herself so that we help each other heal, while moving toward a deeper level of understanding and unconditional love.

I began this extraordinary time looking for the way out or through that St. Paul promised God would provide. I know now what it is, and I have known it all along. The way through all our trials and traumas is to hold on for dear life to the Divine Love that permeates and flows through all relationships—with God and the cosmic realms, with the rest of humanity, especially those with whom we are joined by blood or circumstances, with the animal, plant, and geologic kin-doms, and with all of creation. While one of my mantras still is "Lord, have mercy!," the other is "Love is patient, love is kind," to draw once more from St. Paul's words. Many times I have uttered these words through gritted teeth and can't tell you how many days

I have relied on the grace of God to get us through them, but Love finds a way to penetrate even the deepest darkness and the strongest of human wills.

There have been bright spots during this time, although Tom's condition has not improved much and the quality of medical care he has received is substandard. My own health is much better, thanks be to God, as the effects of the harsh chemo have mostly worn off over two years. I was able to get off all the additional meds I had been given for the various side effects of chemo, and my blood tests confirm that I am a two-year cancer survivor.

While Southern California doesn't yet feel quite like home, I have found much to be grateful for. I am working with a friend I met here on a spiritual book project and some gratifying healing work. I've met others with whom I gather weekly for prayer and reflection and make monthly jaunts into the high desert to a Benedictine monastery, where my new spiritual director resides.

After my extended year of extraordinary time, I am less likely to make plans and anticipate that what is likely is what will happen. I live more in the present than I have since childhood. I place my full trust in God and in little else. Perhaps I finally am living that *Suscipe* prayer in surrender rather than in constant striving toward holiness. My thoughts take me more and more often into the realms of light where those who have crossed through death and are experiencing the afterlife dwell. It is now time to close this section in which I shared the story of my extraordinary time and move into ongoing reflections on what those experiences may reveal to us about suffering, healing, death, and the afterlife.

Part 2: Reflections

FIVE

Suffering

THE PERIOD FROM MY colon cancer surgery to moving to California was almost exactly one year. So fast-paced and chaotic was this extraordinary time that it was simply not possible to reflect deeply on any of what happened until after it was well over and I had had some time to recover. When you ride the roller coaster all you can do is hang on for dear life and pray. Or scream. I did that once or twice. Afterwards, when your stomach stops churning and your feet are safely on the ground, you can begin to assess the damage and the impact of your traumatic experiences. Still more time must pass before you are able to get enough distance and perspective to perceive and accept the many ways in which you and your world have changed.

Once settled in Riverside, I began the daunting process of interpreting that year. I approached my extraordinary time as a living text. Wrestling with challenging texts and extracting meaning from them has been a lifelong endeavor for me, first as a literature scholar and academic, then as a pastor who preached weekly, and more recently as a Benedictine oblate whose go-to spiritual practice is *Lectio Divina. Lectio*, the art of divine or sacred reading, is that complete prayer practice consisting of selecting and reading a text daily, usually Scripture, listening deeply for a word or phrase that lights up for you or shimmers through that text, then meditating or reflecting on its meaning for you at this time, allowing prayer to emerge from the meditation, and finally to rest in silent contemplation as the text continues to reveal itself to you in whatever way the movement of the Holy Spirit may invite. The word or phrase may stay with you throughout the day, as you continue to ruminate with it. Some passages have a way of continuing to open themselves to you like blooming roses over time, in what we call sustained *Lectio Divina*.

I had pondered for months the Scripture passage from First Corinthians 10:13 I led with in Part 1 about God providing the way out of what life throws at us so that we are able to endure its ordeals. Another sacred text for sustained *Lectio* came forward for me during my extended reflections on the extraordinary time, again from one of St. Paul's letters. I had studied Philippians extensively during second-year Greek in seminary but now found new meaning in this passage: "For to me, living is Christ and dying is gain. If I am to live in the flesh, that means fruitful labor for me; and I do not know which I prefer. I am hard pressed between the two: my desire is to depart and be with Christ, for that is far better; but to remain in the flesh is more necessary for you. Since I am convinced of this, I know that I will remain and continue with all of you for your progress and joy in faith."[1]

Like Paul, among the most cherished in my Communion of Saints, I go back and forth between being ready to move through death to eternal life with Christ or to remain here to finish the work I was given following my husband's death: to care for my son and prepare him for life without me, to help a friend bring his important work forward to the public, and to produce this one more book, however traumatic it may be to revisit the events of that year, in order to support others going through trying circumstances. May this be "fruitful labor" in the remaining time God gives me on this earth. And may I always be open to God's leading, wherever it may take me.

The beauty of *Lectio Divina* is that the process of reading, meditating, praying, and contemplating may be applied not only to Scripture and other sacred texts, but also to art, music, poetry and literature, the natural world, and one's own life. While Scripture, icons, and Gregorian chant are perhaps the purest expressions of holy written texts, art, and music, just about anything is raw material for *Lectio*. The habit of sacred reflection, when practiced consistently, takes root and contributes to a fuller understanding of God's love for us and all of creation and a deeper desire to express that love in all that we are and do.

In this and the next three chapters I want to share the fruit of my own and others' reflections on the great human themes of suffering, healing, death, and the afterlife from the perspective of one whose Christian faith

1. Phil 1:21–25.

has been strengthened through my engagement at an intense, experiential level with the playing out of these themes in one concentrated year of my life.

Nearly three years have passed since the events I recounted in Part 1 began. While I'm sure I will continue to extract meaning from my extraordinary time for the remainder of my life, my sense is that I need seriously to engage reflectively in this work now, while I still can recall viscerally my experience of it. One of the most effective ways we heal from such intense trauma to the body, emotions, and spirit, as I will present more fully in the next chapter, is to defuse and release traumatic energy and associated pain while retaining the memories for what they can reveal to us.

Suffering and I have been well acquainted since childhood. A shy, introverted child of nine, my secure world was torn apart when my sixteen-year-old sister, Nancy, was killed in a car accident. Nancy and I had been close, and that abrupt, permanent loss rippled through my life for a great many years. One effect of the trauma was that I experienced magical thinking: I would die in a car accident and/or wouldn't live past sixteen. I realize now that my intimate connection with my sister provoked an emphatic response to her fate. No one helped children process their grief and anxiety in those days, and I stuffed mine down deep. Finally, during some extensive sharing in a pastoral counseling class at seminary forty years later, the dam broke, and my unresolved grief surfaced and got released. Afterwards, I experienced the deep peace of Christ that comes when we allow him to enter into our pain and suffering and heal us.

Given this early experience and many others since, I believe that I have received a gift from the Holy Spirit of empathic suffering. Empathy is about feeling what another being feels at a visceral level. I don't necessarily feel others' joy, but their sadness and anxiety—yes. Because it involves so much pain to feel another's anguish, I sometimes block it to keep from being overwhelmed. When empathy is not blocked, it naturally leads to compassion—"suffering with"—and to action that aids the other. The compassion of Jesus was like that, as we see in John 11 when he travels to Bethany after his good friend Lazarus has died. He weeps with Lazarus's sisters, Mary and Martha, over this devastating loss. The text says that "he was greatly disturbed in spirit and deeply moved."[2] Then he raises Lazarus from the grave. When I am able to suffer empathically it is the Christ within

2. John 11:33b.

me who loves like that and feels the pain of each of us and of the anguished world.

Suffering is not something to compare. It is not accurate or helpful to say that I suffered more or less during my extraordinary time than anyone else in similar circumstances because the nature of suffering is so personal to each of us. We know through faith that God in us is suffering along with us and enables us to suffer with and for others, but it is our own experience that deeply roots this suffering and makes it real.

I mentioned earlier that one subject of sacred art on which I have done *Lectio* for the past few years is the *pieta*. Although this image of Mary holding her dead son on her lap is not scriptural, it is not hard to imagine that it happened after the deposition, the removal of his body from the cross. Christians worship a suffering savior. Catholic churches retain the crucifix as a visual focal point in their sanctuaries, while for Protestants the empty cross signifies that Christ is risen. To me, it's not an either/or but a both/and. Yet where my mind and heart go first is to the suffering Christ and to his mother who stood silently at the foot of his cross holding him in her heart as his life expired.

My mother passed on to me her small sculpture of Michelangelo's famous *pieta*, his *Lectio* on Mary's suffering and the cruelty of the crucifixion. I keep it in my prayer space. My mother carried that image of the broken body of her own child through her lifetime, as Mary must have done. What got Mary through the crucifixion and aftermath was her complete trust in God's promise that her son would rise again and the redemptive nature of his suffering. My mother believed in that promise, too. Now, when I do my own *Lectio* with this image and that of the Bellini *pietas*, I am often moved to tears and experience again the deep-seated abiding pain of losing one's beloved to death. If you love, you suffer. Love suffers with, for, and because of the beloved. Grief is the price of loving, something I explore more fully in the chapter on death. Christ's death on the cross teaches us to not be afraid to love, that perfect love casts out fear. And, I would add, perfect fear casts out love.

How might we learn to endure suffering? What spiritual purpose or value does it have? I'm certain every saint in the Christian tradition, as well as many living women and men, could offer testimony based on personal experience to inform a deeper understanding of the question of suffering. First we must learn to move beyond what is known as the theodicy question: if God is all powerful and all good, why do bad things happen to people, especially good people? Why do people suffer? Why doesn't God intervene and save this child or that group of people? If we can't get beyond this question, can't find an acceptable answer, we are unable to develop a mature understanding of who God is and how God loves.

When my sister died, my father struggled with this question. Why did God take his beloved first-born child from our family? He was confused, angry, and miserable in his grief for months afterward. He even left the church for a time because he couldn't fathom how a loving God could allow such a thing. Later, he made peace with God and within himself, as he recognized that God had been present with Nancy and those who loved her throughout this ordeal. Loving presence is what we may expect from God and those whom God sends to us as our angels and Communion of Saints during these traumatic events.

When my extraordinary time came around decades later, I had learned from my experience of life and of God that the answer to the theodicy question is "why not you?" God doesn't promise that we won't suffer great loss and pain. Only that Love will accompany us through it. Love reaches out to uphold us when we are being tossed about by life circumstances. So "Why me?" was never my question. My prayer was that God would show me how to transform suffering into healing and fear and anxiety into greater trust in God's mercy and love.

During this trying time I did extensive *Lectio* on the book of Job. While I don't wish to elevate my own trials to those of this righteous man of faith, I did observe that Job was stuck on the theodicy question, asking God why he had been stripped of all that gave his life meaning—except for his faith in God, which is, after all, the point. When we are emptied bare of our egos and what spiritual guides call the false or lower self, our essence is revealed as our holy connection with the God who made us and loves us. So also is revealed our absolute dependence on the grace of God. Job's error, and ours, is the expectation that because we keep God's commandments and consider ourselves good people we should be continually blessed above others and not endure great suffering. God moved Job through the dark night first of the senses and then the more advanced dark night of the spirit, when he felt abandoned by and terrified of God. Ultimately, Job became a man of deep humility, fully understanding his absolute dependence on the mercy and love of God. At that point his suffering becomes transformational, and he is gifted with a new life even more blessed than before. Such are the gifts of God when we emerge from our trials by fire.

To further illustrate the purpose and value of transformational suffering and add depth and breadth to our understanding, I offer the experiences and *Lectio* of three brilliant lights of the Christian tradition: the fifteenth-century English anchorite, Julian of Norwich, the nineteenth-century French Carmelite, St. Therese de Lisieux, and Fr. Francis Kline, a Cistercian monk from our own time, who wrote in a profoundly moving way about his own experience with suffering as a path to holiness.

It was not uncommon among the vowed religious through the ages to pray for the gift of suffering as Christ had suffered for love of us. It was a way of showing one's devotion to him and desire for a closer union with Christ through the sacrificial act of suffering. It was also for these Christians rooted more in their personal experience than in theology or doctrine.

While Julian is not yet a saint among the Catholic constellation, she is certainly part of my Communion of Saints. I have admired for many years this extraordinary mystic who enclosed herself in a cell adjacent to Norwich Cathedral. Her cell had three openings: one through which material goods could be passed for her simple needs, one that looked into the cathedral so that she could participate in daily Mass, and one that opened to the street so that people could receive her spiritual guidance. I've always imagined this window with a sign saying, "The doctor is in." Like the *abbas* and *ammas* of early desert Christianity, Julian was a conduit of the Holy Spirit, refined through years of solitary communion with Christ, who was sought out for her words of wisdom. She was a living example of the wisdom of that desert saying attributed to Abba Moses, "Go, sit in your cell, and your cell will teach you everything."

What is most astounding to me about Julian is how in her *Showings* or *Revelations of Divine Love* she revealed the fruit of her labor of *Lectio Divina* for more than twenty years on the meaning of her mystical visions of the suffering Christ. In what is known as the Short Text, she recorded at the time the sixteen visions she received in 1373. Later, in the Long Text, the full meaning of these unfolds through what her *Lectio* revealed to her understanding. The visions were brought on at her own request for three graces from God: an experience of Christ's passion, a severe, possibly mortal, bodily illness, and the three wounds of contrition, compassion, and longing for God. She wanted to suffer with Christ in the way that others who had loved him, such as Mother Mary and Mary Magdalene, had done. All of this was granted her through the grace of God. I cannot do justice here to what may be learned through reading and meditating with Julian's

Showings. What I offer are just a few of her most significant insights on empathic suffering.

In the Eighth Revelation in the Long Text, Julian speaks of how Christ showed her in vivid Technicolor the final moments of his passion, as he approached death. She reports in this stark revelation that his broken body reached its worst pain as his flesh lost its fluids and became dry. This was when, Julian tells us, he spoke the words recorded in Scripture, "I thirst," which she understands on both the physical and spiritual levels. Here are her words:

> This revelation of Christ's pains filled me full of pains, for I know well that he suffered only once, but it was his will now to show it to me and fill me with mind of it . . . I felt no pain except for Christ's pains, and then it came to me that I had little known what pain it was that I had asked, and like a wretch I regretted it, thinking that if I had known what it would have been, I should have been reluctant to ask for it. For it seemed to me that my pains exceeded any mortal death . . . . Of all the pains that lead to salvation, this is the greatest, *to see the lover suffer* [italics mine]. How could any pain be greater than to see him who is all my life, all my bliss and all my joy suffer? Here I felt unshakably that I loved Christ so much more than myself that there was no pain which could be suffered like the sorrow which I felt to see him in pain.[3]

Julian goes on to observe that Mary's pain was greater than all the others who loved her son because she was so united to him in love. "Here I saw a great unity between Christ and us, as I understand it, for when he was in pain we were in pain, and all creatures able to suffer pain suffered with him,"[4] she astutely remarks. The whole creation was suffering with him, except for those who did not recognize him. Paradoxically, Julian looked to the cross for comfort and safety, saying that "I would rather have remained in that pain until Judgment Day than have come to heaven any other way than by him."[5] His union with divinity not only enabled him to "suffer more than all men could" but "gave strength to his humanity" to endure that suffering: "I saw that the love in him which he has for our souls was so strong that he willingly chose suffering with a great desire, and suffered it meekly with a great joy." Pain turns to "everlasting joy by

3. Julian, *Showings*, 207–9.

4. Ibid., 210.

5. Ibid., 212.

the power of Christ's Passion."[6] Christ helps her to understand that "the suffering was a noble, precious and honorable deed, performed once in time by the operation of love"[7] and that if he could have suffered more for the redemption of the world he would have done it. At the end of *Showings*, Julian summarizes the spiritual understanding she has gleaned from her intense visions, ongoing colloquy with Christ, and years of reflection: "Love was his meaning. Who reveals it to you? Love. Why does he reveal it to you? For love . . . . So I was taught that love is our Lord's meaning."[8]

Empathic love or compassion, then, is grounded in the Divine Love that unites all of creation through Christ and his redemptive suffering on the cross. If one is a follower of the crucified one, suffering for his sake and that of others he loves is always part of our stories. For me, that empathic love through which I felt my husband's pain of diminishment for many years and finally his suffering death, and the constant psychic and physical pain of my son that I still experience with him most every day, are reflections of the pain Christ suffered for and with us. And it is all an emanation of his Love.

This doesn't mean that all suffering is redemptive or even necessary. Some we bring needlessly on ourselves through poor choices. More is caused by forces beyond our control. But how we respond to our own suffering is as important to our spiritual growth as how we respond to the suffering of others. It sorely tests us at all levels of our being and asks, at times, more of us than we can begin to imagine. Yet suffering is always strewn with gifts offered through the grace of God that, if we recognize them, are transformational.

One of the many gifts of my own time of intense suffering was learning how to receive what others wanted to offer. As someone who had considerably more experience with giving than graciously receiving, I was grateful to be instructed by the loving-kindness of friends, family, and even strangers. From the volunteer who repaired the garage door mechanism at my New Jersey home to the ones who drove me to my medical appointments to those who sat with me in the hospital or comforted me at my husband's funeral to the friends who dropped off hot meals when I couldn't cook, many people came to my aid, even without being asked. I will always be grateful for them and the sympathetic understanding and empathy that

6. Ibid., 214.

7. Ibid., 217.

8. Ibid., 342.

motivated them to act with compassion in my time of great need. How would I ever have known of the depth of their love without giving them such opportunities to minister to me? It was surely of mutual benefit. Ever since I have found it much easier to receive these loving expressions as well as to offer them without expecting anything in return. Love freely given is beautiful.

Another gift of this time, particularly of that period during which I had trouble swallowing and spent long hours alone in my house, was that of deep, nourishing silence. It was a silence forced on me by my circumstances and my husband's death, broken only by the need to respond to the occasional phone call or knock at the door. At times it was terrifying, as when I was choking on my meal or unable to move because of my fractured back, but ultimately I recognized, paradoxically, that the enforced silence was freeing. It was at some level a relief not to have to communicate every thought or feeling, and I began to sink into silence and welcome it as the desired mode of the contemplative I once again allowed myself to be.

During Lent this year I revisited the subject of silence in the Christian contemplative tradition. The Rule of Benedict encourages inner silence as a means of listening for God's invitations and for discerning how and where God is leading us. Deep listening frees us from the compulsion to speak or to formulate our next thought while listening with half an ear to what someone else is communicating. In this way it is linked with the practices of humility and obedience to God's desires for our lives.

I found increasingly that the silence fed my spirit, that the noise around and within me began to fade, and I could begin to hear my own heart beating in time with the rhythm of the universe. In an odd way, it was like being on retreat. The first few days of a retreat require us to empty ourselves of all the intrusive voices within us so that we can experience true silence. Ultimately, the mystery that is the deep wellspring from which we draw our being waits there, hidden from us until we seek God's presence. There we can rest in silent contemplation, in trust and acceptance, like the weaned child resting on its mother's lap in Psalm 131. Contemplation, the fourth part of *Lectio Divina*, is, sadly, one of the most overlooked and little understood practices of our Christian faith. The Centering Prayer movement has contributed to making it a central spiritual practice for many, but it truly belongs with and completes our *Lectio* as we seek sacred presence in our daily lives.

Many of those on the spiritual path are familiar with St. Therese of Lisieux, the nineteenth-century French "Little Flower," who, though she died at twenty-four, left a mighty legacy through her practice of what she called "the little way." She also suffered a most horrible death by electing not to receive treatment for the tuberculosis that ravaged her young body and caused excruciating pain, which she endured without complaint.

In her autobiography, *The Story of a Soul*, it is clear that Therese was highly sensitive to an extreme degree, feeling things more intensely than those around her and suffering as a result. My son is also one of these highly sensitive people, so I recognize his nature in hers. Apparently, about 15 percent of the population could be called "highly sensitive," myself among them. Anxiety and nervous conditions are common with this group. The young Therese goes to great lengths to enter at the tender age of fifteen a Discalced Carmelite community, where her older sisters also resided, in order to lead a cloistered life of prayer and contemplation.

Like Julian, Therese, in her colloquy with Jesus, asked to suffer and to convert her suffering through small sacrificial acts to love and healing of others. After three years at the Carmel she can say, "I see that *suffering alone can give birth to souls*,"[9] and quotes John 12:24, where Jesus speaks of the grain of wheat that must fall to the ground and die so that it can produce new life. Later she reveals that "I don't desire suffering or death . . . and yet I love both of them. But it is *love* alone that draws me . . . . For a long time I desired them both, I possessed suffering, and I thought I was touching the shores of heaven. I thought that the little flower would be gathered in the springtime . . . . Now it's abandonment alone guides me—I have no other compass!"[10] Still, she desires to be the victim soul consumed in the fire of divine love whose sacrifice is accepted as an offering and transformed into relief of the suffering of the world. Since she sees herself as a little soul, she offers little acts of self-sacrificing love to God, such as trying to love an unpleasant noise that one of her Carmelite sisters constantly made. This kind of "little way" is within the capacity of all of us, to give of ourselves in ordinary, loving ways without resentment or calling attention to what we are doing. If we are able to offer acts of kindness and generosity in little ways, we move beyond suffering even when we are asked to give ever more of ourselves and what we hold dear for the love of God.

Therese of Lisieux has become a popular and appealing saint because we can identify with her and her method of strewing these little loving flowers as she moved through each day. She is not an intimidating saint,

9. Therese de Lisieux, *The Story of a Soul*, 197.
10. Ibid., 202.

until you look more closely at how much she physically suffered in her dying. Her physician couldn't understand how she bore the pain of her debilitating disease. Her lungs were dissolving from the tuberculosis. Yet as she lay dying she is said to have spoken of not being able to suffer any more, that suffering was sweet to her as it would carry her to Christ. Her physical anguish was transformed by her beloved into the highest expression of her love for him.

Fr. Francis Kline offers his own dying as a path of holiness in his final work, published as *Four Ways of Holiness for the Universal Church Drawn from the Monastic Tradition* in 2007. I was privileged to have met and spoken with Abbot Francis on two or three occasions when I served as an associate pastor at First Presbyterian Church, Hilton Head Island, South Carolina. Abbot Francis's Cistercian (Trappist) community, Mepkin Abbey, was located near Charleston, not far away, and was a holy, serene place to make a retreat. The abbot was a Juilliard-trained organist, and Mepkin had just renovated the chapel and purchased a new organ for him to play for the glory of God when I first went there. Offering his gift of sacred music to God was a way of praying for Abbot Francis and a rare privilege for the community and its guests to hear. Though, like Benedictines, Trappists follow the Rule of Benedict, they are a more contemplative reform of the older order and follow a strict *horarium* punctuated by seven daily prayer liturgies and assigned work. *Ora et Labora* circumscribes the life of these abbeys. It is important to keep this in mind, as we consider the nature and degree of Fr. Francis's suffering.

Four Ways of Holiness includes a profound essay entitled "Suffering," in which Abbot Francis speaks of the holiness of suffering by sharing his own experience of it and his *Lectio* on that experience during the nearly two years from the onset of his illness until his untimely death at fifty-seven. He begins by saying, "Suffering disperses and fragments the energies of mind and heart into a thousand points of light and makes reflection on it a hazardous task." He speaks of calling upon *Lectio Divina* to "gather around and reunite me into the reception of an illuminative message" of his experience of God, which he defines as "the urge we feel when God is breaking in on us at mind, heart, will, or anywhere in our person, so that we, in the context of faith, are able to respond to him, immediately or eventually, in prayer and action." His intention is "to penetrate as deeply as I can the experience of suffering I have undergone and continue to undergo, so as to clarify for myself what God is doing to me, in me, and for me."[11] It is this account of God's action within Fr. Francis as he experienced it that I found especially moving and profound. It certainly illumined much of my own experience, especially the stripping away of parts of myself I had thought essential.

Suffering, whether primarily physical or emotional, diminishes us in a number of ways. I will speak more of these in the next two chapters, but here I want to mention several losses I experienced also enumerated in Fr. Francis's account and common to all who suffer. The primary loss is, of course, of one's life. In my case I did not suffer this, although I was taken to the brink often enough to empty me of all desire but for God's mercy. In my vulnerability, it made me more dependent on God and more able to trust in God's merciful love. The loss of life I experienced was my husband's, and that was devastating enough. Loss of capacity was huge for me, as my physical deterioration took place over the course of the year. Loss of significance, which often accompanies aging, was a component of my suffering, as I could no longer support the roles I was used to playing of teacher, spiritual leader, and wife. Loss of stability was a hard one, too, as I had to leave my home, family, friends, church, and way of life. In the Benedictine tradition, stability is one of the three vows taken by those entering this monastic order, stability of place and also of heart. I would confront this loss in some depth over the course of my extraordinary time. And I have just illustrated how the loss of my voice for that period of time during which I could not swallow led to deep reflection on the meaning of silence.

In Fr. Francis's case, symptoms of illness led to a preliminary diagnosis of chronic lymphocytic leukemia, thought to be manageable if not curable. One of his first experiences of suffering was feeling that he and his community were under siege from well-wishers who found out about his illness and wanted to help. At that point he felt illness was personal and private. Remember, he was a contemplative introvert who spent much time in prayer and in community life. That was about to end. Sent to Sloan-Kettering in New York for a second opinion, he was told he could be monitored several times a year. But he could not shake chronic fatigue, compounded by stomach problems. When next he went to New York for a checkup, his doctor was alarmed at his condition and hospitalized him. Reading Fr. Francis's description of sharing a room with someone who had

11. Kline, *Four Ways of Holiness*, 25.

company 24/7 and kept the TV on loud activated my deep empathy for this monastic stripped not only of his health but also his community, his daily *horarium*, his music, his administrative duties as abbot, and even of silence itself in which to contemplate his condition. Over the next year, he was to spend endless weeks in the hospital while being pumped full of antibiotics to control his constant fever and low white-cell count. Loss, loss, and more loss in the manner of Job. He had to cede control over his environment as well as his body. This was familiar ground to me. Still, he was able, because of long years of contemplative practice, to create spiritual space for himself even there and spoke of the ascetic practice of being still and quiet which was given to him as a gift of Spirit. From his hospital room he could see God's sunrise, a daily joy, be cared for by kindly nurses, and practice the spiritual discipline of patience.

Fr. Francis's condition continued to deteriorate. His veins were poked several times a day for infusions, and the antibiotics could not control the constant fever. He experienced the painful separation of being away from his community and of missing important monastic functions at which he considered his presence indispensable, losses of connection and significance. He adapted because he had to and began to see himself as a sick person. Yet he looked for more spiritual consolations, which came in the form of the Eucharist brought by chaplains and priest-friends to his room daily and to visits from his confreres, bringing news of the community.

His physician now believed that his disease had transmuted to lymphoma, not easily treated. He reflects that as the connections with the world as he had known it were cut off one by one, something opened for him: "the narrow gate of suffering . . . . Suffering at the invitation of God, I concluded, admits into us a new life and a warmer love. Long had I been preparing for this. Long had I dreamed about it. Now, it had been mine, only not mine but given as an invitation in the most unlikely of desert places, a semi-private hospital room." He cried out to God as Jesus had done in the garden of Gethsemane "to deliver him from the chalice of pain."[12]

At one point Fr. Francis grieves the loss of his capacity to play the organ for God, an especially huge loss for him. He still had music in his head but in the absence of playing now also was able to listen deeply to the silence. This is a gift I shared with him in my own illness. There is a certain spaciousness, almost a leisure that opens as an invitation to thought and contemplation as one's schedule is cleared of all but rest and alone time.

12. Ibid., 45.

For me, the silence was healing. For Fr. Francis, as the weeks and months passed, it gave him the space and time to accept that he was dying.

At an especially low point, when his nurse couldn't find his vein for an IV, he "wept and lifted up my heart and mind to God, and what I found was Christ crucified, and not my pain any longer but his. Could this be some kind of union? Though still in agony, I knew that I was comforted, not physically but spiritually, because I was privileged to be at that kenosis that saves us all."[13] His words are reminiscent of those of Julian and Therese.

Finally, he felt that God was teaching him perhaps the deepest lesson of all, that there are no limits to suffering. "The pain, of whatever kind, is the key to opening the door. It makes us need God, who wants to be needed . . . . It builds endurance and character. It creates a new kind of hope, based solidly on his love for us and for others . . . . The only way forward is to wait on God, and continue to endure, for that is what our life is, in union with Christ . . . . I wait anxiously for the day to accept the invitation that will come to take the hand God offers and go through the door of death."[14] That day was soon to come. As for my husband, the way through the suffering for Fr. Francis was death.

Before he passed away in the late summer of 2006, Abbot Francis was returned home to Mepkin, which now became a place of hospice. Visited by a friend, he told him something I have been pondering since I read it: "I love God. And I love what God is doing."[15] I love what God is doing, he could say as he prepared for his transition to eternal life, emptying him of all but his essence, the pure point of his eternal union with God.

The author Flannery O'Connor, who suffered from an incapacitating form of Lupus, was attracted to the concept of "passive diminishment," which she came across in the writings of Pierre Teilhard de Chardin, the great twentieth-century Jesuit priest and geologist with cosmic vision. According to O'Connor, passive diminishment is "the serene acceptance of whatever affliction or loss cannot be changed by any means."[16] Elsewhere she spoke of how "our spiritual character is formed as much by what we endure and what is taken from us as it is by our achievements and conscious choices."[17]

13. Ibid., 54.

14. Ibid., 62.

15. Ibid., 157.

16. O'Connor, *The Habit of Being*, 53.

17. O'Connor, *Spiritual Writings*, 109.

I have found this to be true. The spiritual practice of self-emptying or *kenosis* is the intentional stripping away of all but the essence of self, what the Trappist writer and mystic Thomas Merton called "*le point vierge,*" that pure, holy, inviolable essence that is our eternal connection with the Christ within us and around us. Christ on the cross, stripped of everything but his capacity to hand his will over to God, in the greatest *Suscipe* prayer of all time, is the model. What happened to me in that extraordinary year and to Fr. Francis as he approached death is along those lines. We may not have chosen to go there, but once there we can choose to accept it in that act, paradoxically, of passive diminishment, because we cannot change the outcome. Just as Therese of Lisieux could say on her deathbed that she no longer suffered because suffering was sweet to her as she handed over her life to Christ and Francis Kline could say that he loved what God was doing in and with him, what makes suffering purposeful and valuable is its conscious acceptance, along with what we relinquish for the love of God and others, chosen over our own perceived well-being. We receive our true well-being when we willingly surrender our bodies, our wills, our minds and hearts, and our eternal souls to God even as they are taken from us. I believe this is what Julian of Norwich learned from the words of Christ she passed on to us: "All shall be well and all shall be well and every good thing shall be well."[18] If we fully trust in that, even as we enter into death, that final journey to God, we have free will to choose to accept this passage to our true home. And what passes to God at that moment is that pure, holy essence of our God-given selves. We have been given no more profound gift than this, nor have we any better one to give back as we cross over into death.

Once during my ordeal I heard in meditation, "Embrace suffering as a sacrifice of love" and "Love doesn't count the cost." Julian, Therese, and Francis knew this and practiced it, and the fruitfulness of their lives and their *Lectio* have left a grace-filled legacy for the rest of us. Nevertheless, transformational suffering is not an easy path to holiness but rather the narrow gate of which Jesus spoke as a way to the kingdom of God. As I said to my then-spiritual director, Sr. Theresa, now suffering from a dread terminal illness herself, "Some days it feels as though Satan is sifting me like wheat." Without pausing, she responded, "You're being made into bread for others." Maybe so, I thought later, but I didn't think I'd be kneaded so often and so hard!

18. Julian, *Showings*, 149.

SIX

Healing

JUST BEFORE MY EXTRAORDINARY time began I had planned to write a book about healing within the Christian tradition. I own over one hundred books on the subject, have trained with several gifted healers, and have practiced healing ministry for going on twenty years. Did any of this prevent me from getting cancer? Was my choice to undergo a regime of toxic chemotherapy consistent with my understanding of how the human body heals? Did my experience with healing enable me to grieve my husband's death with more grace than if I had no special knowledge? The answer to all of these questions is a qualified no. I do not know definitively how or why the colon cancer showed up. It could have been genetics, environment, and/or a metaphorical expression of unresolved grief or other deep-seated emotions. As for the chemotherapy, I explained earlier my reasons for electing to undergo it despite my concern for its harmful effects to my body and well-being. And grief, however prepared we think we may be for the loss of a loved one, will always surprise us in how and when it grips us, despite what we know about its common patterns.

Healing is a complicated, nuanced subject, one I know more about than when I prepared to write the healing book a few years ago, but the how and why of it remains an enigma wrapped within the profound mystery that is God. Just as Job's ordeals moved him to deep humility and gratitude before the Mystery, so too have mine. Instead of the book I had planned, I will share with you here what I have come to understand about healing, especially from within the Christian tradition.

Let's begin by stating boldly that God's desire is for us to be well and whole in body, mind, emotions, and spirit. Always. And yet sickness and death entered our world because of human choices, some made long ago and passed down through the generations, and others made for us or by us in our own time. Now we deal with genetic anomalies, like mine; family miasmas, like patterns of abuse or proclivity to alcoholism; toxins we ingest not willingly, as with my chemotherapy, but through air, water, and ground pollution from industrial waste; and acts of violence toward our fellow humans and creatures. Add to these human-caused issues like accidents and natural disasters, and we have a short list accounting for most of the illness and injury in our world.

That doesn't mean that any one of us necessarily will succumb to Parkinson's disease or PTSD, Alzheimer's or ALS, earthquakes or floods. True, research can tie some causes or proclivities to specific illnesses, such as lung cancer from smoking or liver disease from alcohol abuse, but cause and effect is neither linear nor discoverable in many situations. In any case, God is not about blaming the victim, nor are we. Why some people or animals contract or are able to recover from dread diseases or serious injuries and others are not isn't simply a medical issue. It's part of the larger mystery. We do know a great deal now about how to take good care of ourselves and our families through nutrition, exercise, adequate sleep, reducing stress of all kinds, and, most importantly, through nurturing healthy, mutually loving relationships that are reflections of God's love for us. And, as we have seen, becoming ill or injured does have a gift side. That's redemptive love at work.

On our behalf, God may employ many instruments and avenues of healing, including the very broad fields of conventional, allopathic medicine, as well as alternative modes both ancient and modern, as varied as acupuncture, music therapy, spiritual energy healing, and prayer. Again, it's not an either/or menu of healing modalities from which we must choose, but rather a both/and menu. God has gifted researchers and scientists, doctors and medical personnel, psychologists and therapists, and healers of many varieties to offer healing and help restore us to wholeness. Our cultural backgrounds and belief systems usually dictate which items on the menus of modalities come first, last, or not at all. Having explored and experienced a wide range of these over my nearly seventy-five years of life, I have developed a sense of which are more efficacious and tolerable for particular people and circumstances. Then too, I have committed myself to following Christ and accepting the wisdom of the Christian tradition in all things, so what I offer here is deeply rooted in my observations and understanding of how, why, and whom Jesus healed.

For heal he did. Nothing was more central to his ministry. More than twenty percent of the Gospels is devoted to accounts of his healing. His prophetic teaching challenged many, but he won people's hearts through restorative acts of healing. People flocked to him to be healed of demons and diseases and stayed to listen to his teachings. When Jesus healed he brought the kingdom of God directly into people's lives. Those healed and those who observed these unexpected, miraculous healings witnessed the in-breaking presence of God. Then, by teaching and empowering his disciples to offer healing and at Pentecost bestowing the charism of healing upon the apostles, the body of Christ which became the church was gifted with the capacity to offer God's healing love to whoever would welcome and receive it.

Healing in the Christian tradition is a hallmark of the reign of God. But since the word *healing* has many meanings, it may be helpful to sort these out. Healing is not necessarily the same as curing. In the Hebrew Scriptures and the New Testament we find nuanced meanings of "to heal." The Hebrew word *rapha* was the most common biblical word for what might be translated as "to make whole" or "heal." Traditionally, the Archangel Raphael is known as the agent of God's healing: *rapha* for healing and *el* for God. Other Hebrew words denote aspects of healing, such as cure or remedy, wholeness and soundness, and restoration to health. The Hebrew greeting "*Shalom*" means complete wholeness, harmony, and peace among all, much the same meaning as in the expression "Peace be with you," commonly used in Christian worship to embody fellowship and reconciliation.

The messenger Archangel Gabriel transmits to Mary at the annunciation God's chosen name for Jesus, *Yeshua*. It means "savior," "healer," "deliverer," or "he saves." So from his conception Jesus is designated as the savior, healer, and deliverer of his people, one of a long line of prophets like Moses and Elijah before him who received the charism of healing. Jesus' gift of healing was used in his ministry to deliver the people of God from their greatest enemies—not the Romans who conquered them, but the dark forces of sin, evil, and death.

In New Testament Greek, several words translated as "healing" have more specific meaning. *Sozo* is more likely to mean "made whole" in the sense of saved, protected, healed, and preserved, than *hugies*, which usually refers to sound health. *Therapia*, the word from which "therapy" derives, is a treatment leading toward wholeness, while *iaomai* may be translated as physical and sometimes spiritual healing. *Egerin* meant to restore health, even from death. How these words are used in Jesus' healings nuance the meanings of these occasions. Similarly, in English we may speak of cures on the physical level but of holistic healing as wholeness of the entire entity: mind, body, emotions, and spirit. We are enfleshed spirits, so wholeness means much more than a physical cure. We may be healed of afflictive thoughts and behaviors or of the power of emotional hurts, for example, without being cured of physical ailments. Through faith in Christ and the power of the Holy Spirit we are forgiven and saved from sin and death, although we find varying interpretations of the understanding of salvation through the centuries and within the differing faith communions.

While Jesus healed people of their physical limitations in every instance reported in the Gospels by also healing their emotions, minds, and spirits, he restored them to wholeness. Only this complete healing enabled them to resume their places in the families and communities from which their illnesses had separated them. Think of the hemorrhaging woman isolated for twelve years, the Gerasene demoniac now "clothed and in his right mind," or the ten untouchable lepers. He restored them to the full *Shalom* of the kingdom of God, a foretaste of what is to come for all of us when the reign of God is fully established once more on earth. No wonder the Gospels and the book of Acts feature healing so prominently among the actions of Jesus, the disciples, and the early church!

One of my favorite healing texts is found in Acts 3. Peter and John are entering the temple to pray, when a man lame from birth asks them for alms, for charity, since he could not support himself. Peter looks at him intently, then offers him his hand with these words: "I have no silver or gold, but what I have I give you; in the name of Jesus Christ of Nazareth, stand up and walk."[1] The astonished man not only walks but leaps for joy at his restoration to health, praising God and making sure all those in the surrounding area know of this miraculous gift. Peter uses the healing as an opportunity to evangelize the amazed crowd. Healing proves again to be a most effective means of turning people's hearts and minds to Christ. The power of Peter's words always gives me the sacred shivers when I hear them. By the way, the book on healing I was going to write would have been titled *What I Have I Give You*.

1. Acts 3:6.

How might we reflect on the meaning of these powerful healing texts today? I want to suggest that we expand our understanding not only of what constitutes healing and wholeness but also of the many ways in which people can be assisted in recovering their well-being. It is well known in medical and alternative healing circles that disturbances in the emotions and spirit, in particular, often end up manifesting in the physical body. It is possible that my cancer originated in emotions and blockages stemming from as long ago as my childhood. Although an anxiety condition was exacerbated by the chemo, it also could have been attributed to a whole host of issues occurring in my life during that extraordinary time. Were my swallowing issues a result of my not being able to swallow what was happening to me and my family? In his fascinating book *When the Body Says No: Understanding the Stress-Disease Connection,* medical doctor Gabor Maté effectively makes the case that many illnesses, diseases, and conditions result from undue stress on the whole self. By the time these appear in the body, they usually have been present in a person's energy fields for some time. Yet allopathic medicine is ill-prepared to help patients recover from any but the physical symptoms, which is usually all medical doctors are prepared to treat.

As an example, a few months ago I experienced severe, ongoing pain in my left hip. This affected my daily activity, like walking my dog, which I was unable to do for several months. Both Tyler and I were gaining unneeded weight! When the hip pain didn't clear up, I saw my primary care physician, who, after briefly moving the leg and hip, declared it was arthritis, for which he was willing to prescribe anti-inflammatory drugs and recommended Ibuprofen several times daily. My intuition was that he was wrong, and I declined the drugs. I then waited weeks more to see an orthopedic specialist, who, after a twenty-second examination of the motion of the hip and leg, concluded that I had bursitis. His remedies were a cortisone shot and pain meds. Again, I declined treatment. Having had positive experiences in the past with osteopathic manipulation, I contacted a doctor of osteopathy who came highly recommended. Although I had to wait weeks for an appointment, it was worth it. Three sessions with him and my problem cleared up. The treatment? Lying on a table while he manipulated tissues and tendons with his fingers. No medications were offered or needed. He noted that my right hip was out of alignment by a half inch, which had caused my problem. Neither of the other physicians had offered a cause or a lasting remedy. In between sessions with doctors,

I rubbed holy anointing oil on my hip and prayed for relief and healing. I have been pain-free for many months now.

You can see why I am skeptical of conventional medicine, which treats body parts without regard for the whole person. Tests, meds, and surgery have become tools of allopathic medicine. Specialists have replaced generalists. My husband's experience in the hospital after his fall showed the glaring flaws and gaps in conventional medicine. My son's experiences with the medical system have been little better. Mention the word "doctor" in his presence, and he will complain at length of his treatment at their hands. I have seen enough of the Medicaid system available to the disabled to largely agree with him. While I appreciate the sophisticated tools medical doctors have at their disposal, which have saved countless lives, they cannot heal some of the more common maladies of our time, like post-traumatic stress disorder and more generalized anxiety.

Thankfully, other options are available to us that can contribute to holistic healing—which brings us back to the kind of healing offered by Jesus. His style of healing was not a matter of form or technique but rather of loving relationship. His intentions were always for the highest good of the persons he healed, and it didn't matter whether he spat and made mud balls to spread on the eyes of a blind man or touched a leper. People were healed just by being in his presence and opening their hearts to God's love through him. Jesus could also heal at a distance, as was the case with the Roman centurion's servant. Love was both the motivation and the energy that healed, and that is still true today. Many believe that Jesus could heal because he was the son of God but that that charism is no longer present in the contemporary church. Yet we are taught by Scripture and our faith traditions that the gifts of the Spirit have been given to the church not just at Pentecost but ever since.

Jesus showed us how to prepare ourselves to offer words or acts of healing to others. Those whom he healed for the most part first were invited to receive healing, like the man born blind in John 9 or the paralytic at the pool in John 5, whom he asked, "Do you want to be healed?" Not everyone does. Some, like this man, don't take responsibility for their own healing or settle for a diminished existence. Others took the initiative to seek him out, like the hemorrhaging woman who touched the hem of his garment, or the ten lepers. Some he healed almost despite themselves, perhaps because their healing was needed for the greater good of the community, like the Gerasene demoniac, the Samaritan woman at the well, or Zaccheus, the tax collector. Study of and reflection on the healings Jesus performed can help us understand how we might offer healing to others. So also can the history of the healing practices of the church.

As early as the Epistle of James, mid- to late-first century, the specialized role of church leaders in healing began to be demarcated: "Are any among you sick? They should call for the elders of the Church and have them pray over them, anointing them with oil in the name of the Lord. The prayer of faith will save the sick, and the Lord will raise them up, and anyone who has committed sins will be forgiven."[2] Note the connection between sickness, suffering, and sin, which is central in Scripture. Sin, whether individual, generational, or communal, leads to sickness, suffering, and death. But praying, the laying on of hands, and anointing with sacred oil become powerful remedies of the community. These simple acts of compassion, forgiveness, mercy, and love in the name of Christ transmit healing energy and blessing to those ready to be healed. They form the core of the church's lay ministry of healing through the ages, the pastoral care of the sick.

For the first eight centuries of its existence, this vital ministry of healing was commonly practiced by the laity, empowered by baptism and the charismatic gifts of the Spirit. While the oil used for anointing was typically blessed by the priesthood, healings by deacons and the community using the oil were widely practiced. By the early middle ages, sacramental power began to be concentrated in the hands of priests and taken out of those of the laity to ensure its use in accordance with the church's teachings. Throughout the first millennium of the church, however, the understanding that the health of the body and spirt were intertwined was retained. Only in modern times did the separation of these begin to affect the practice of medicine. We are beginning to see centers of alternative medicine arise even within conventional hospital settings, as proponents of managed care recognize that prevention and holistic therapies are far less expensive and destructive to the body than surgery and chemical solutions.

Up until around the fifth century, when monasticism replaced desert spirituality in the West, the desert *abbas* and *ammas* were often approached for their capacity to heal. They cast out demons and healed diseases for many who sought them out for their holiness. Later, medieval monasteries became places of healing. The twelfth-century Benedictine abbess, Hildegard of Bingen, designated a saint and Doctor of the Church for Roman Catholics in 2012, was one of the church's most gifted healers. She

2. Jas 5:14–15.

used herbs, nutrition, and sound therapy among her tools of healing. As the practice of the laity offering healing to the sick through anointing with holy oil began to be phased out, the anointing of the sick and dying became a sacrament in the Catholic and Orthodox churches. Another significant shift from early church practice happened when anointing and laying on of hands with prayer for any who were sick were limited only to those believed to be dying. The sacrament of Extreme Unction, or Last Rites, as it formerly was called in the Roman Catholic church, could only be offered by priests under prescribed circumstances and only once.

Following the Second Vatican Council, that sacrament's roots were sought and found. They go all the way back to Jewish tradition which the priests of Jesus' time practiced, and the church began to restore anointing to a more sacramental role in the whole life of the church. Now the sacrament of the Anointing of the Sick is for anyone who wishes it and is available more than once. Healing services including anointing, laying on of hands, and prayer are offered in many churches across the denominations. I personally have attended many such services in this country and elsewhere in the world and offered them during my pastorate. In my view, weekly or monthly healing services would be a blessed supplement to any faith communion's ministries.

Sacramental churches, such as the Roman Catholic, Orthodox, and Episcopal, also offer relief and support for mental, emotional, and spiritual suffering.

The sacrament of Reconciliation, for instance, in the Catholic church includes confession and penance leading to forgiveness and restoration of wholeness. Through confession, we acknowledge how we separate ourselves from God's love and turn again to Christ for forgiveness and reconciliation with those we have hurt. The sacrament does offer considerable power through God's unconditional love and absolution. In addition, the sacrament of the Eucharist, at the heart of our faith, is the remedy and means of reconciliation with God and among the people of God. Through partaking of the body and blood of Christ, we are redeemed, united with him, and made whole through his sacrificial death and resurrection. The Eucharist, signifying the divine graces of forgiveness, mercy, reconciliation, and love, makes healing through the power and intercession of Christ available to all who believe in him. This essential sacrament offers healing for the soul, and, along with baptism, is the communal celebration of the redeeming love of God and the sacrificial death and resurrection of Christ.

Instances of sickness—emotional, mental, and physical—that are resistant to conventional treatment can benefit not only from the healing sacraments and services mentioned, but also more particularly through two effective modalities which may be offered within the church or alongside the church by people trained in these ministries. These are intercessory prayer and spiritual energy healing.

The first and most common is intercessory prayer, simply praying to God, Christ, and/or the Holy Spirit for another's healing or well-being. We do this routinely, in our personal and communal prayer. Next to asking for help for ourselves, asking God to intervene on behalf of others is the most common type of prayer. We may know those we pray for, or we may ask God or the saints to intercede for categories of people: the sick, the homeless, the poor, victims of violence and injustice, nations, or causes, for example. Our prayers may take many forms, from free-flowing to liturgical, such as litany during worship, pastoral prayers offered on behalf of congregations, rosaries, novenas, prayer vigils, and the like.

One may well ask why intercessory prayers are needed, if God knows our every need and wants the best for us. Something about the energy and frequency of intercessory prayer affects those prayed for, and it also changes us. Studies of intercessory prayer, such as those Dr. Larry Dossey presents in his books on prayer and healing, show positive results, and many hospitals and clinics now encourage prayer for patients. Dossey, a cardiologist, spoke at my invitation a number of years ago at a church in Santa Fe, where he lives. His scientific and pastoral perspectives have added much to the body of literature on the subject of healing prayer.[3] I remember once, as a pastor, asking the congregation to pray mightily for the healing of a former parishioner who had been badly injured in an accident. He was not expected to fully recover his functions, even if he lived. A compromised life for this college president in his fifties with teenaged children was not to be imagined. So we prayed together mightily, as many others were doing. Over time, he recovered. We don't know why prayer works; we just know and trust it does, in whatever way God chooses.

When praying for healing we don't necessarily ask for a specific outcome, as we did in the above example, but rather for God to remember the person and to heal in whatever way God desires. I'm not sure it is any more or less effective than being specific, but it does respect the person's

3. See Dr. Dossey's earlier books, *Healing Words* and *Prayer is Good Medicine*. His later work, *One Mind*, deals mainly with consciousness studies.

free will in the matter, which God also respects. Asking a person how to pray for him or her is advisable, although we also learn to trust our own intuition and how Spirit leads us. Like many people, I keep a personal list of those I care about and those in special need of prayer for whom I try to pray daily. Categories of people also are important to remember, even those for whom we do not have natural compassion, like perpetrators of violent acts or terrorist groups, who are perhaps more in need of prayer than those we love.

Praying for someone or a group, holding them up in your own remembrance and God's, is a mutual gift. In so praying, we develop deeper ties to and compassion for those for whom we pray and with God. Praying through saints and angels are also common practices of the faithful. We are inviting one or more of our Communion of Saints to intercede with God on our behalf. All saints, at least those so designated by the Catholic Church, have had healing miracles ascribed to them. Some recent ones with strong charisms of healing, such as St. Pio, known as Padre Pio, or the Blessed Solanus Casey, both Capuchin friars, performed many healings during their lifetimes and were sought out by thousands for the ways in which Christ worked miracles through them. A good friend of mine was the recipient of one such healing from Padre Pio when he was an infant. I will say more about the practice of praying through saints in the chapter on the afterlife.

Many kinds of prayer ministries exist in churches, from prayer chains when someone is sick, hospitalized, or has died, to Stephen Ministry, which offers one-on-one pastoral care from trained laity. Prayer is often offered in communities of Pentecostals and Charismatics during worship or in prayer groups, accompanied by singing or speaking in tongues.

However intercessory prayer is offered, it is a great ministry of the church to those in need and generally much appreciated by its recipients. However, it is often limited to physical illness. We tend to be more comfortable praying for physical healing than for other kinds of losses, such as broken relationships, job losses, or financial crises. We also tend to put time limits on when we think people should have recovered from whatever they are dealing with, rather than continuing to hold them in prayer indefinitely.

Over the years I have studied the healing prayer ministries of some of the better known recent healers in the Christian tradition, including Agnes Sanford, Dorothy Kerin, Ruth Carter Stapleton, Ron Roth, Benedict Heron,

OSB, Tommy Tyson, and Avery Brooke, all of whom have passed on and, I suspect, are assisting from the other side. I have also become familiar with three significant current ministries of healing: Christian Healing Ministries, headed by Francis and Judith MacNutt, the Linn family ministries, and the Order of St. Luke. In addition, I know well and have prayed with several other gifted healers. From my study and experience it is clear that some individuals have been given a special gift of the Spirit for healing, while others who offer healing prayer are compassionate, loving people who have others' best interests at heart. Both kinds of people are needed in prayer ministries. All of those mentioned above have left legacies of their work in books and training materials.

The Linn family, consisting of Matt, a Jesuit priest, his brother Dennis, and Dennis's wife, Sheila, has produced more than two dozen excellent and very accessible books on aspects of healing, such as the healing of memories, spiritual abuse or addiction, life's greatest hurts, healing through forgiveness, and the especially intriguing *Gifts of Near-Death Experiences*, to which I will refer in the chapter on the afterlife. Matt alone or the three Linns are available to offer healing retreats and trainings, and I highly recommend their work. I met Matt several years ago at a retreat he offered on healing life's greatest hurts, which I found exceptionally beneficial. We have remained in touch since and have prayed together. He would say that all that is needed when offering prayer for another is a loving, open heart and a positive intention for the other's good.

The Linns' work stresses those areas of healing that they consider as unfinished emotional business for so many dealing with anger, anxiety, depression, guilt, and shame. I would add to the list unresolved grief, which can cause or contribute to any of the above emotions. One of the effective ways in which they assist people to heal these emotional stuck places is to invite Jesus to enter into the place of their deepest pain and allow him to share it with them. Many wonderful healing stories have emerged from this simple form of imaginative prayer from the Jesuit tradition. Those who suffer from these unresolved emotions would do well to work with someone trained and compassionate who can support them in this kind of prayer.

Christian Healing Ministries, headquartered in Jacksonville, Florida, and headed by former Dominican priest Francis MacNutt and his wife, Judith, offers four levels of training through their School of Healing Prayer. CHM, whose motto is "Listen. Love. Pray," also works with individual clients in need of healing. They do very fine, comprehensive prayer work with a charismatic or evangelical flavor, and often develop long-term relationships with their clients, staying with them until they have healed sufficiently to continue on their own. Francis MacNutt is now in his nineties and is one of those gifted with the healing charism. He knew several of those now-deceased specially gifted healers mentioned earlier and has written a number of important books on healing, including one simply called *Healing*, which is a good place to start. Judith MacNutt is also gifted and has authored books as well.

The Order of St. Luke is an ecumenical, international Christian organization for healing prayer that has been around for several decades. Those wishing to join OSL begin by studying Jesus' ministry of healing. When ready, they become full members. OSL, to which I belong, is organized by chapters and regions. Most chapters are small, and many are connected with one particular church which offers healing prayer for the congregation and the local community. OSL provides training materials, conferences, and opportunities to join with others in praying for healing. It serves a small niche in the Christian church which could easily grow with wider interest in this kind of ministry and more denominational participation.

One of my own desires is to train people to offer ministries of healing prayer, but the way forward for that is not yet open or clear. Meanwhile, I occasionally pray with a prayer partner for particular healing needs and am open and listening to God's further invitation, if it comes.

The other healing modality I want to hold up, spiritual energy healing, is less well known in the church and sometimes looked upon with suspicion. The reason for that is that most spiritual energy healing practitioners are among the category we call "spiritual, but not religious." I know quite a few who are both spiritual and religious, however, including myself, who either have received the charismatic gift of healing from the Spirit or have developed a practice of working with the body's numerous energy fields to clear and balance them to promote healing. People from other faith traditions and belief systems also are gifted healers, and, just as with intercessory prayer, one's intention, compassion, and love are the most important criteria for working in this field.

Spiritual energy healers seek to enfold the person or group with which they are working in a high-vibration energy field. As in all forms of healing, God's love is the source of this healing energy. A healing session may be carried out in person or at a distance, since consciousness and energy are not confined by space. Particle physics teaches us that energy may exist as material particles, waves of potential, or both at once, even at great distances. I am able to feel such energy around and within myself and usually also of those I'm working with. Often people who do this work use sound, touch, scent, or objects that support healing, such as the Christian sacramentals of anointing oil, holy water, or blessed salt. In my experience, high-vibration energy offered in love acts to break up stuck patterns to release them from the energy fields of the subject of healing. The fields are then rebalanced and sealed to restore and protect the body's natural harmonious flow of its energy centers and systems. From time to time someone is healed in a particular way as a result of the session, and nearly always people leave feeling more peaceful and relieved of stress.

In Christian spiritual energy healing, practitioners call upon Christ and perhaps the saints, angels, and archangels to guide and enable the healing. I see it as a more specialized form of intercessory prayer as well as an offering of a specific spiritual gift. In this form of healing we set aside self-interest or attachment to the outcome in order to allow the healing energies of God to flow through us and work in whatever way God chooses.

People who offer spiritual energy healing are generally trained in multiple healing modalities and often have professional credentials that complement their healing work. Many nurses, for example, are practitioners of Healing Touch, which as a result is more widely accepted in hospital settings than other forms of spiritual energy healing. Sometimes their services are even covered by health insurance.

For those who suffer from PTSD and anxiety conditions, which are often resistant to psychotherapy and are treated with meds, one promising form of energy healing that appears to work fairly rapidly and consistently is the Emotional Freedom Technique, which involves tapping on accupressure points on the face and upper body while reciting statements of affirmation and release. While the painful memories that are triggered in anxiety attacks aren't erased, the emotional sting of them can be significantly reduced through this technique. Dawson Church's helpful book, *EFT for PTSD,* is a good place to start if you are interested in finding out more. I took EFT training years ago, and quite a few energy workers and therapists are certified in this modality.

While I have been trained in multiple forms of spiritual energy healing and have taught it to others, I personally do not offer or accept such healing anymore except in the name of Christ or whomever Christ may designate.

Through experience, I recommend that you assure that whoever works on you is an open, clear, loving conduit of God's healing love, no matter what the practitioner's beliefs. Earlier I mentioned Sr. Pat, the Franciscan sister who offered spiritual energy healing for me while I was so ill. I knew her heart and trusted her implicitly. Her loving work brought me great relief, and after moving to Southern California I received several distance healings from her, which contributed to my recovery. I also know quite a few Catholic sisters and lay people who have been trained in spiritual energy healing who offer it lovingly and prayerfully for the benefit of those who seek their help.

It is unusual for one session of intercessory prayer or spiritual energy healing to produce dramatic results, although I have been present at a number of healings that could be labeled miraculous. The effects of this work are generally boosted through multiple sessions. People are only prepared to release so much in one session. After they become more used to this kind of healing, they are more likely to allow the emotions, traumas, and grief held deep in their energy fields and bodies to release and leave. Inviting Christ or one of his saints who knew such suffering to receive what has been released and transform it into love for the benefit of others is a great way to finish a session.

Loving energy has a positive effect wherever and however it is offered. As people gain experience with this kind of healing, it becomes clear that it is another way in which God is present to heal us.

If we are on the receiving end of intercessory prayer or spiritual energy healing, as I often was during my extraordinary time, we will be inspired to accept these gifts of the love of God expressed through friends, family, and healing practitioners with great gratitude. They can help raise us out of despair and grief, release our anger and lack of forgiveness, and heal our most painful memories. Thanks be to God for those in our own Communion of Saints who care for us and contribute so much to our healing!

SEVEN

Death

THE CHRISTIAN DOCTRINE OF eschatology speaks of four last things: death, judgment, heaven, and hell. As hugely significant as this doctrine is for our faith and understanding, rarely is it presented in ways that offer hope and consolation to those who mourn or are preparing for death. Here I will reflect on the last thing which happens first, death, and the other three which follow in the final chapter on the afterlife.

Between the time I wrote the last words of the previous chapter and began this one, death visited our household again, suddenly and traumatically. Our nine-year-old Golden Retriever, Tyler, who has been so much a part of the story of my extraordinary time and of my life before and since, died a few days ago. Grief is fresh again. I had nearly forgotten how visceral it is, how it feels physically, but I remember now, and it makes these reflections on death all the more wrenching, yet timely to write.

Tyler was as much angel as dog. He was my constant companion, my shadow, and kept the whole household on his preferred schedule: breakfast at 6:30, dinner at 3, followed by a walk, feed the cats at 5:30 so he could lick the cans, last time outside at 8 PM, then half the night downstairs, and half upstairs, arriving in my room around 3 or 4 AM to announce his presence, then nap until it was time for me to get up and tend to his needs. He had an infallible sense of timing and would stand and look at me expectantly if I didn't honor this schedule or his claim to a treat. The recent change to Daylight Savings Time threw him—and me—off for a few days, but then he got right back to work keeping us on Tyler Time. He reminded me of a monastic keeping his daily *horarium*. Tom is as broken-hearted as I am, and even friends and family who knew our Golden boy mourn his loss with us. "Tyler, Prince of Dogs," we called him, and that he surely was—a gift of God, a big, handsome bundle of love freely given, never withheld, no matter what. Last night I awoke around 2:30 AM, certain that I heard him breathing in his sleep on the rug beside my bed. I listened for several minutes to this familiar sound, which stopped when I sat up. Was that a visitation from my sweet boy to comfort me while I slept? Wherever Tyler is now, I trust he is free of pain and in a good place, surrounded by love as beautiful and unselfish as his.

I will soon explore more fully the concept and nature of the afterlife and what I have come to understand about what happens after souls of people and beloved animals pass through death. Here I want to consider death itself from the perspectives both of those who pass through its threshold and those left behind. I will wrap around these perspectives what Scripture and the Christian tradition teach us about the meaning of death.

I begin with the perspective of those left behind, because I have been one of these most of my life, beginning with the traumatic death of my sister, followed by companion animals, parents, several close friends, my beloved husband, and now Tyler.

When death is sudden, traumatic, and unexpected, there is no time to prepare for that wrenching departure, and grief is often delayed. In the case of the death of my sister, it was forty years before I was ready to consciously grieve her loss and release the pain connected with her passing. When Alden died, I was so ill and traumatized by the suddenness and magnitude of his death that I hadn't the strength to grieve. Paradoxically, I felt weighed down with grief or perhaps from holding it back. It wasn't until several months after the move to California that I had the space and time—almost the luxury, I want to say—to allow the deep sadness to bubble to the surface and spill into my daily life. Slowly that began to dissipate, as I accepted that Alden was now in a place without pain or fear and that I could still find some meaningful work, new friendships, and even occasional joy in life without him.

However you try to postpone your grief until you are ready to deal with it, grief will not wait until you decide to acknowledge that it's there. It creeps up on you and attacks, overwhelming your emotions and physical being, so that it can't be ignored. Missing the presence of the loved one and being startled into realization that he or she is gone is constant in the first days and weeks of grieving. I entered the kitchen from the garage yesterday after returning from a day at St. Andrews Abbey, the Benedictine monastery in Valyermo, California, where I go each month to meet with my spiritual director. As I opened the door I expected Tyler to be there to greet me, as he always was. The longer I'd been gone the more exuberant his greeting. Jumping up to put his paws on my shoulders meant "I thought you'd never get back. I missed you! Where's my dinner?" That's the kind of greeting I expected but had to face that he wasn't there and wouldn't ever be again, and it was just too painful to go there. To lose yourself in grief just takes too much energy and too much time to recover from. It hurts the heart and takes its toll on the whole body.

In his well-known book *A Grief Observed*, about his own stages of grief following the death of his beloved wife, Joy, C. S. Lewis compares grief to physical pain: "At worst the unbearable thought only comes back and back, but the physical pain can be absolutely continuous. Grief is like a bomber . . . pain is like the steady barrage . . . with no let up."[1] His book was begun when his grief was raw, and he records how it changed over time. He reflects that he thought he could "describe a state, make a map of sorrow. Sorrow, however, turns out to be not a state but a process. It needs not a map but a history."[2] That feels so true. Deep grief like his is the price of loving well and being loved. All of us will pay it at one time or another and, likely, multiple times. By the end of the book, Lewis is able to realize two significant gains that came through his grieving process. He is able to turn back to God, after blaming God for Joy's death, and he is able to remember her without all of the emotional pain. He finds peace in both these gains. His experience is fully human and his capacity to write of it full of grace for those of us who suffer the loss of loved ones and want to grasp at the hope that the peace he describes will come. If it doesn't, then the grief needs more time and perhaps a fuller and guided process from a qualified professional or spiritual director.

No one's process is the same as anyone else's. Neither is the timing at all the same. We must not expect ourselves or others we care about to be through the worst of grieving within six months or a year. Part of the reason for an extended process is that often grief is attached to other deep-seated unresolved emotions, such as guilt or shame or anger, that unfinished business mentioned earlier. Healing the memories, especially if traumatic, is necessary in order for the grief process to proceed to a more peaceful state. The practice of forgiveness may be essential in the process to find

1. Lewis, *A Grief Observed*, 57–58.
2. Ibid., 76.

relief from the pain of grief if blame given or accepted is involved. Excessive grief is in a way denial of the love of God, which always leads through death to hope in eternal life. Trusting that the loved one has been received by a merciful God is essential for good grieving, yet the possibility that suffering or separation from God continues after death is something with which many are concerned for themselves or their loved ones. I'll say more when we reflect on the afterlife. Here I just want to stress that God's love and mercy are without limit, so we can never assume the worst possible scenario. It adds to our own suffering and diminishes the promise of hope.

The ancient Christian doctrine *prolixitas mortis* or "the dying life" suggests that death is not simply an event that ends a life but that we experience loss, suffering, and sickness throughout our lifetimes and that these can all feel like death. They are in fact a kind of death.[3] The process of dying that Fr. Francis Kline experienced and wrote about with such poignancy and beauty is an expression of this dying life. Any time we are deprived of or deny ourselves something we have believed essential to our well-being or survival, like his lengthy absence from his monastic community, we experience this *prolixitas mortis*. As eminent theologian Karl Rahner put it, we experience a little death every time "something perishes that the person judges to be possible, realizable, and desirable, and yet he is deprived of it."[4] Each time this happens it requires a deeper surrender to the inscrutability of God's will.

The losses I enumerated in previous chapters which occurred during my extraordinary time and afterwards illustrate that little or partial deaths precede our actual physical death and present us with opportunities to choose faith over fear, hope over despair, and love over separation. Ultimately, our faith calls for us to choose Christ in full freedom only by that moment when we actually die. Any time up to or before that moment is better, but the final moment is ultimately what determines whether we truly belong to him. Jesus confirmed this in his promise to the "good" thief who died next to him on the cross that he would that day join him in paradise.

But since we cannot know our hour of death, it is perilous to wait until the last moment to claim Christ as our Lord and savior and to confess where we have fallen short and receive forgiveness. When we are close to death, as Alden was in the hospital, we are rarely in a position to make a

3. See Rahner, "Prolixitas Mortis," 226–56.
4. Ibid., 231.

full and free choice. The Catholic Church's Last Rites or Extreme Unction, replaced since Vatican II by the sacrament of the Anointing of the Sick, was exercised when death appeared imminent so that the dying could go to heaven confessed and absolved with Christ's name on their lips at their last breath.

One of the losses I experienced at Alden's death was that of being a wife, of being married. In a culture which strongly values being coupled, becoming suddenly single or widowed is part of the shock of death and was certainly one of those "little deaths." I had never thought of myself as a widow, yet that's what I became to a considerable part of society. The mail I receive from Princeton University is marked by a "W" signifying that I am the widow of an alumnus. Social Security also classified me as a widow, entitled to widow's benefits, such as they are. This new identification of me as a widow was disconcerting, to say the least. It defined me as someone bereft of a husband, which I was, but confined to a lower social status than before.

The Old Testament pairs widows with orphans as those most in need of community support. In several passages in the New Testament letters, it is made clear that widows were sustained at the public expense. Their daily needs were to be attended to as the "widows' right." According to a letter St. Augustine wrote in the early fifth century known as "To Proba,"[5] there even seemed to be an order of widows with enrollment required: the widow had to be sixty or over and to have lived a useful and charitable life. It contains quite extraordinary instructions for widows on what was expected of them. They were to pray without ceasing, exhibit exemplary piety, and not engage with the affairs of the world. Their models in Scripture were Mother Mary and Anna, the prophet-widow in Luke 2, who lived in the temple and prayed night and day. Many saints of the early and medieval church were widows who founded charitable or religious orders after the untimely demise of their husbands. These exceptional women set a pretty high bar for the rest of us.

At one point I looked up the word *widow* to discover its derivation and meaning. From various sources, it seems to have derived from being bereaved or solitary and lonely. Its dictionary meaning is simple: a woman whose spouse has died who hasn't remarried. While some women may think of themselves as a "football widow" or "golf widow" because of their husband's devotion to some interest other than them, I was the plain,

5. Augustine, "To Proba."

ordinary kind and remain so, yet I have not been able to identify with any of these limited definitions of myself. Since I always had a professional life apart from my husband's, I didn't suffer from the kinds of isolation many widows do, nor even from the stigma of being widowed. I certainly didn't expect to be supported by the community because of my new status. It was my emotional loss that changed me far more than my legal or financial status. My husband had been my constant companion and the love of my life for nearly three decades. I did feel bereft of his presence, companionship, and love. I still do. No one ever appreciated me as much as Alden did or was as interested in hearing about my daily activities. And no one will ever call me out again in the way he had a right to do.

On the list of desolations, losing your life partner is at the top. The daily intimacy of living together and constructing your lives around each other's desires and needs is over. When "we" became "I," this newly uncoupled "I" had to sort out how my future life would take a different turn from how and where "we" had chosen to live.

Through the discernment process that involves sorting thoughts and options until the one to which the Holy Spirit is guiding us becomes clear, I found that Alden's death also necessitated another kind of radical change in lifestyle. This resulted in the move to California and living in a wholly new set of circumstances with an adult son who envisioned a vastly different kind of life for himself. Now my identity is not only that of a widow but in his eyes an elderly mother for whom he feels he must assume caregiving duties. The solitude I experience in this new life is of a different kind from before, and I seek out friends who share my faith and generational values so as not to feel isolated. Trips to the monastery here and St. Ben's in Minnesota help. Were it not for the commitment to my son, I would probably seek to live the life of a claustral oblate within the monastic community.

Whatever direction my future may take, widowhood is mine, and I had no choice in the matter. In the *Lectio Divina* group I meet with weekly, two of the other six women have become widowed since I have. Now I see them going through similar processes and identity shifts, trying to figure out how to be on their own, perhaps for the first time in their lives. Losing a spouse or longtime partner is comparable to no other kind of loss, because of the unique quality of intimacy that is shared in such relationships and no others. Grief opens an empty, hollow space within that no one else can fill.

When I was ministering in Hilton Head, South Carolina during my first pastorate, I performed several weddings of couples who were remarrying late in life. One octogenarian was tying the knot for the third time, his bride for the second. To me it seemed the triumph of hope over reason. From my widow's perspective, I now can better understand that need for companionship that leads people to seek another mate, even though I wouldn't want to go that route.

When the loved one who died is a child, the loss must be the most excruciating of all. This is what I see in Mary's face and body language in the Bellini paintings of the *pieta*. It is not only unexpected but unnatural that a child should predecease her or his parents. For those I have known who have lost a son or daughter to death, there is lifelong grief. Even if there are other children, the one who passed away is always counted when telling the number of their children.

I remember one seminary classmate whose older brother had died, and his parents' grief had been passed on to him, as he was considered by them and accepted himself to be the "replacement" child, conceived to replace the one who had died. How sad, I remember thinking, to carry such a burden through life. In a way, I carried something similar. I was the youngest of three girls. The oldest died at sixteen, the middle child disappointed my parents' expectations, and I became the one appointed to carry these out. "Let me have one in three," my mother would pray, when I failed to perform in some way. So I was the one who got the advanced degrees, married well, had a successful academic career, and produced a gifted son. Except that things didn't follow the long-term script, and most of my middle-aged years were spent dealing with the losses that followed each of these "successes." I experienced those "little deaths" many times over.

You would think that those experiences would have sustained me through my extraordinary time, and in a way they did. Yet when faced with the crush of so much pain and trauma in such a short space of time, it was not so much my experience that provided "the way through" St. Paul identified, but rather my faith. Nothing happens in God's universe without a higher purpose or without God's love sustaining us. Knowing I could count on that, even though I couldn't make sense of it all at the time, was my saving grace. Surrendering to and trusting in the love and mercy of God helps us survive these little deaths and also prepares us for our eventual cessation of life on earth, as we saw with Fr. Francis Kline.

Sickness is a herald of death, even when we escape its clutches, for in it we often are helpless to affect the outcome, and so come to understand that living with the inevitability of death is our fate as humans and as Christians who accept death as the gateway to eternal life, through which we are led by the crucified and resurrected Christ.

Preparing to leave the world and making peace with God and with others is an essential part of our spiritual journeys, so let us now turn to focus on the one who is departing this life and how he or she may experience what is known in our faith tradition as a good or happy death.

In Chapter 4 of the Rule of Benedict, monastics are advised to keep death always before their eyes, not only as a reminder to live a holy life, as death may take us at any time, but also in order to remember our hope in what awaits us on the other side of death. St. Benedict became known as the patron of a happy death, as he died with his arms outstretched to Christ to receive him. A traditional prayer to Benedict for a happy death asks the saint to pray that we may receive the graces he did to never be separated from Christ and to be received into his arms at the hour of our passing through the veil of death.

Neither my sister Nancy's nor Alden's death was expected. Each was taken suddenly and experienced fear and pain at the moment of death rather than the quiet, even joyful passage that many have been granted through God's grace. It is pointless to question why that was so. Certainly, God didn't love them any less, and we can be sure that at the end of their passages they were greeted lovingly. In the Christian tradition, the martyrs and saints are presented as our role models, those who lived holy lives and were able to surrender them to God as acts of faith, hope, and love in the face of evil and even the most painful of deaths. We saw this in St. Therese of Lisieux and in Fr. Francis Kline, as in the depths of his suffering he could say, "I love what God is doing," preparing him for the ultimate surrender and the ultimate loving union.

Reflecting on the traumatic deaths of those closest to me and extending these thoughts to a wider circle—all those who leave this earth with unfinished business—I wondered how these departings might have been peaceful, no matter the circumstances. It seemed to me that only if we are prepared to go gently into that good night instead of raging against the dying of the light, to paraphrase Dylan Thomas, might we experience a death that is truly the consummation of our lives rather than a wrenching ending. If we are ready and willing, as in the *Suscipe* prayer, to surrender our lives that completely to God at any time, then whenever death comes we face it with courage and grace, as it delivers us from further suffering and assures us that Divine Love will enfold us at the moment of our passing and forever after.

The closest example of a happy death in my personal experience was the passage of my good friend Meg. I spoke earlier of how when she knew that she would pass from cancer and while she still had the capacity to do so, she called together her closest friends and laid out with us her desire to leave with her affairs in order and be reconciled with any dear ones from whom she had been estranged. She wanted to spend several days with each of us at the end to share our deepest love for each other and to help her carry out some of the tasks she needed done, like distributing her possessions to charity, with personal gifts specially chosen for each of us. She also made sure to prepare her mother and sister so that they could visit as they were able and complete any expressions of love and acts of forgiveness still remaining.

I had five lovely days with Meg a month before her passing. We had said all that needed to be said and spent a couple of evenings watching her favorite Christmas movies and letting the tears come as they would. When I left her, it was with overwhelming gratitude for the gift of her friendship and this precious time of holy retreat. The veil had been thin for her during those days. She had heard an organ playing and a heavenly choir singing familiar hymns from her Episcopal upbringing, and she could read the thoughts of those around her. It was clear that death was fast approaching. Hospice helped her make the crossing a few weeks later, and by then she was beyond the capacity for speech or organizing the distribution of her worldly goods or relationship-mending.

The grace of a lingering death like Meg's is that of time to do what is necessary to experience a good death. Not everyone receives that gift, but another kind of happy death I have encountered takes place in monastic communities and religious orders. I have attended several sisters' funerals at St. Benedict's monastery and have observed much to admire about the Benedictine way of death. The way the body is lovingly washed and prepared by her sisters, the communal wake that precedes the funeral, the picture of the sister with a burning candle before it in the dining room, her constant remembrance in the prayers of the community, the beautiful liturgy of the funeral Mass with special care given to music and homily, the solemn procession to the cemetery where her body or ashes are committed to the ground, with each person participating in covering her casket with earth—all these rituals have been offered for centuries.

I have often thought how comforting it must be when facing death to know that when you pass from this life to the next you will be ushered out with such loving care and remembered forever after on the anniversary of your death, your "Feast Day," at prayer. And how consoling to know that your remains will rest in those pleasant grounds marked with the distinctive cross that signifies your place in this long chain of sisters who lived, loved, and worked in this wonderful monastic community.

The Benedictine way of death highlights how important funerals and memorial services are when someone we loved passes. At all times in all cultures, these funerary practices were deemed necessary not only to comfort the mourners but to properly and respectfully send off the departed on the next stage of his or her journey. When these kinds of rituals are poorly observed or not at all, people often have a sense that closure is missing or that they didn't honor the life of the deceased.

My friend Christine recently lost her sister to cancer discovered too late. While neither her sister or brother-in-law were believers, Christine's Catholic faith is strong, and she prayerfully chose to hold a Month's Mind Mass, a requiem Mass held one month after a death, in her parish church. It was a beautiful service attended by more than fifty friends and family, followed by a reception. The Month's Mind Mass was an especially good choice since traditionally it was held for those who remain in one's mind and heart a month after their death. The people who came to honor Christine's sister expressed gratitude for the closure this service brought them. Community rituals are important, especially in the face of death and mourning. Choosing the appropriate one for the circumstances is too.

If you have strong feelings about what you want or don't want to go on at your funeral, be sure to write down your wishes and communicate these to your family. When I planned Alden's funeral with his Lutheran pastor, I knew not only what he would want but also what was appropriate for such a service, as I conducted many funerals myself when in the ministry. One memorable one came shortly after I had taken my first solo pastorate. The son and brother of prominent church members had died of AIDS. This was more than twenty years ago in a conservative community. What to say, especially since I hadn't known the one who died? I spent some time with the close family finding out about the young man who had passed, what he loved and how he spent his time, so that I could deliver his eulogy. The Presbyterian order of service was well suited for the occasion, and we added lovely music to lift the spirits of those grieving this death. Afterwards, the family and church members were grateful that the occasion was tastefully and respectfully handled and that the focus had been on the young man's life and the Christian hope of the resurrection, not the manner of his death.

I wonder how many people fear their deaths. Is it most of us? Or is that fear concentrated more among those who don't believe in an afterlife they may look forward to? Most people I know well acknowledge fear of how they might pass more than where they are going afterwards. They fear pain, trauma for themselves and loved ones, and being taken suddenly without warning or preparation. Naturally, they fear dying alone. I certainly did during my extraordinary time. No one wants to think that they might pass unnoticed from the scene and not be found for days. That is truly a fate worse than death! In cities where people live isolated lives and aren't known by their neighbors, this happens more often than we might think. An article in the *New York Times* just this week spoke of this phenomenon. Loneliness in life leads to a lonely death. T4he importance of supportive community throughout our lives cannot be overemphasized.

Although Alden died suddenly, I believe he accepted that it was his time. In fact, I know he preferred it to the prospect of living a life of further diminishment and decline. He would not have tolerated well having to stay in rehab for weeks or months while his hip healed. My sense and that of close family is that he was ready to go, to relinquish his life rather than live in misery or cause it for his loved ones, chiefly me. That doesn't exactly constitute a happy or peaceful death, as we would have desired, but he reached beyond his fear to what was the best outcome for himself under the circumstances.

Death always brings consolations as well as desolations. It often brings welcome relief from pain and trauma, draws people closer together as they share the loss of a loved one, and allows for transitions that couldn't have happened otherwise. All of those surrounded and followed Alden's death. It was also an opportunity for many who had known him over the years to pay tribute to his life and for his children and grandchildren to share their cherished memories of him and to express what they had loved about him. While the blessings that come with death may be difficult to see in the first throes of grief, we generally discover and acknowledge them over time.

If we can conceive of such a thing as a happy death or dying well, what might constitute that for each of us? Dying peacefully at home in old age with our loved ones gathered around us may be the ideal, but experience tells us that that rarely happens any longer largely because of cultural changes and lack of religious involvement. Hospice services offer compassionate care to those about to depart and support to the family caregivers but are not a substitute for the kind of preparation we all need to make to have even the possibility of leaving this life with peace of mind and offering that to those we leave behind.

Dying well seems to me to require three essential things: faith that death is not only an end but a beginning; healed, loving relationships; and leaving a thoughtful legacy. Of greatest importance is starting with the knowledge or at least the faith that death is a transition rather than only a finality. Yes, it marks an end to our lives on earth and to all that we had hoped for and feared during that life, all that we had loved and desired and accumulated and cast aside. We can't minimize its significance. What we will experience after death will be far different, as we shall see. For Christians, hope in an ongoing life with God after passing through death is foundational. As St. Paul put it, "If for this life only we have hoped in Christ, we are of all people most to be pitied."[6] Our hope is built on God's promises and faithfulness and the witness of those who experienced the resurrected Christ. There is much to look forward to, and if our faith is strong and sure we need not fear even the passage through death.

For people who don't share that faith and hope or who believe in another kind of afterlife or none at all, surely sufficient scientific and spiritual evidence exists that our consciousness survives our physical death to satisfy even the most skeptical. One source of that evidence can be found in the many accounts of near-death experiences that have appeared in recent years. These NDEs have come to be widely accepted, even by the medical profession, and give us fascinating glimpses into the realms beyond this one. I will explore these experiences more fully in the final chapter. For now, these occurrences in which people pass through clinical death and then return to life with vivid memories of those moments during which their consciousness was separated from their bodies provide some of the most compelling evidence that death is not the end of our existence.

Those for whom that is a terrifying thought rather than a consoling one perhaps have some unfinished business to tend to before they pass beyond this life, bringing us to our second requirement for dying well. What kinds of issues require our attention? Are there relationships that have been important in our lives that are damaged or have been ignored?

---

6. 1 Cor 15:1.

What steps can be taken to repair these now before it's too late for one or the other of us? What would it take to get us to begin those steps?

For many years my living sister and I had issues. I resented her for taking so much of my parents' time, energy, and money supporting her and her children from three marriages. I felt neglected and had little compassion for her and how difficult her life had been. For her part, she resented the quality of life she thought I enjoyed and knew little of my struggles through the years. Finally, about a decade ago, I started returning to our hometown, Detroit, every month or so, offering healing work there and serving on the board of a community development nonprofit. I felt hypocritical doing spiritual energy work when my sister and I were estranged, so I intentionally began to call her and take her out to lunch during those visits. It wasn't long before we both confessed to our hidden resentments of each other over the years. Both of us were surprised by what the other had felt and sorry we hadn't cleared things up years ago.

We have forgiven each other for both our real and imagined slights through the years and now enjoy a mature, loving relationship. Both of us have had major health issues, are recently widowed, and are living with a son, so we have more in common than we had for years. Even though we rarely see each other, as I don't get back to Michigan very often and she can't travel, we know that we love each other and that our different lifestyles and interests can't separate us anymore. I am so grateful that God brought us together in this way and enabled each of us to appreciate the other. I enjoy hearing her memories of our childhood, which have filled in many blanks for me. What a tragedy if one of us, now both in our seventies, would have died before our reconciliation! Scripture is clear that we are to love one another the way Christ has loved us and that if we bring our gift to the altar but have not reconciled with our brother or sister to leave it immediately and heal the broken relationship.

Part of my commitment to living with my son is to help him heal from his years of suffering from anxiety, failed dreams, and a painful separation from his father. As indicated, although it hasn't been easy, we are making progress and are more tolerant of each other's different personalities, interests, and values than we were when we were younger and in a different kind of relationship.

One of my highest priorities is to maintain good relationships with those for whom I care. That doesn't mean it's easy. I like to communicate more often than some friends and family members. Thankfully, social media gives us more opportunities to connect across the years and long distances. "Liking" something one of our grandchildren has posted on Facebook maintains the connection even when phone calls or personal visits are rare. Since nearly all of my remaining family and friends live far from me, email has become an indispensable way of keeping in touch, as phone calls are often hard to arrange.

Sometimes we have broken relationships with those who have already passed on. I believe that it is still possible to heal these through prayer and the healing of memories as well as through "safe" conversations with the dead in which we express our feelings and offer and ask for forgiveness. Several of the Linns' books, mentioned in the chapter on healing, can help with this essential work.

A third significant requirement of preparing for a good death is to leave a thoughtful legacy, not only of our material means, but especially of our faith and values. We have had our entire lives to model for and with our loved ones how to live a full, meaningful life. If we aren't satisfied yet with that part of our legacies, then we can identify what needs to change and begin to take the steps to make that happen. This part of our legacy generally ties in with the previous part, healing our relationships and taking responsibility for what we have left undone. At each Christian service of worship we call to mind and confess to God our sins. We ask for and receive forgiveness. It is an essential pattern in our relationship with God and also with the people in our lives, one that calls for constant vigilance, penitence for our past failings, and commitment to becoming kinder, more generous and loving people.

My son once asked me how we Catholics can be absolved through the sacrament of confession for those patterns and actions through which we separate ourselves from God, others, and God's creation, without atoning or making reparations for what we have done or failed to do. He noted that the criminal justice system requires those convicted to pay back society and twelve-step programs ask people to contact those they have hurt through abusive actions and seek reconciliation. Why then, he wondered, do Christians consider themselves forgiven by God without making amends or reconciling with those we have hurt? Good questions, and not easy to answer simply by saying that Christ's death on the cross atoned for all sin for all time. Jesus told the woman caught in adultery in John 8, "Go and sin no more."

Through confession we are forgiven through God's grace and mercy but also directed to change our behavior and choices so that we don't continue to harm ourselves and others. Yet because of our human condition, however good our intentions, we will fail again and suffer and cause suffering again and again. God's mercy is unending, no matter how often we fall short, yet as we consider what constitutes a good death, surely a clear conscience or peace of mind, as Alden used to put it, is a priority. What would it take to make amends as best we can or to release those unresolved emotions we have carried too long? While Catholics receive penance following confession, it is rarely more than a few prayers or some time in communion with Christ before the tabernacle containing his consecrated body. That is well and good, but sometimes not even contrition or tears of compunction are enough to remove our guilt and shame and sense of regret. And sometimes the people we have the hardest time forgiving are ourselves. As we shall see, full accountability will come after death, but while we still have time we might prayerfully consider how to remove the emotional and spiritual burdens we carry before our passing. Doing so might even improve our longevity!

Related to this is doing what we can to not leave messes for our loved ones to clean up after we are gone. Tom and I were watching the TV show *American Pickers* the other night and commented on how some of the people the two pickers visit are hoarders. Hoarders accumulate so much stuff and are so attached to it that they can't let go even when offered good prices for things they haven't used or even thought about for years. What a nightmare for their families and heirs to have to dispose of when they pass on! I have good friends who have been avid collectors over the years of antiques and various sorts of collectibles. Now in their eighties and in poor health, it is too late for them to organize the auctions or estate sales their children will have to hold in years to come, even before the family home can be sold.

Jesus spoke about the wealthy who build bigger barns and must leave it all behind when their lives are required of them. Being able to detach from all that is not of God is a deep and ancient spiritual practice. We are called to love God beyond all things. One of my favorite cartoons appeared in *The New Yorker* many years ago. A man was standing in his home library with floor-to-ceiling bookshelves stuffed with books and smiling at them fondly. The caption read: "You are all my friends." As a book lover and former literature professor, I identify with that man. I have owned thousands of books in my lifetime and have given away tons of them over the years. My recent move 2,700 miles across the country became a forced exercise in detaching from stuff, motivated by saving considerable money by cleansing my home of most of my personal possessions. Letting go of some of these felt like more loss, as they had good memories of Alden's and my life together attached to them. Yet they needed to go to those who could use them, and ultimately the exercise was freeing. I will, however, confess that my bookshelves here are now full again, like the man's in the cartoon. Books just have a way of growing back on the shelves.

What stuff do we need to let go of before we depart? That may not be a question so much for younger people, but those of us who are older have a responsibility to pass along in this lifetime not only to loved ones but to charity our excess stuff and funds we don't need and even to go beyond this to radical, sacrificial generosity. When asked what he did for a living, Alden used to say that he "gave away Andrew Carnegie's money," since he worked for the Carnegie Corporation of New York as a grant-maker. Carnegie, whom some would call a robber baron and certainly had much to account for in how he made his fortune, still set a remarkable example as a philanthropist, establishing public libraries in small towns across the country and giving away ninety percent of his $300,000,000 fortune during his lifetime. His *Gospel of Wealth* encouraged other wealthy entrepreneurs to do the same. Bill Gates of Microsoft is a contemporary example of that extraordinary level of philanthropy that can make such a huge difference when strategically employed.

Our material goods that don't get passed on in our lifetimes need to be carefully considered and disposed of through an updated estate plan. This has been an area of great concern to me over the years, both in my own family and through encouraging good estate planning for others, including charitable giving. Part of my own unfinished business is trying to ensure that Tom is adequately cared for if I should pass before him, which is the likelier scenario. This is not an easy task under the complex circumstances we're dealing with, but I continue to pursue it and update my estate plan periodically because I know it will give us both tremendous peace of mind if it can be successfully accomplished.

A good estate plan is an act of love, not fear. Disposing of our worldly goods thoughtfully, consistent with our faith and values, providing financial management for those without the skills themselves, passing on a legacy through our charitable gifts, writing out our own desires for burial or cremation, disposal of remains, care of companion animals, funeral wishes, and so on, are all expressions of love and caring for the people, pets, and assets we aren't going to get to take with us. Feeling prepared in this way lessens anxiety and fear and provides comfort for family and friends. Most of us have some work to do in this category, I am guessing. Since I used to help people with their estate planning and charitable giving, I have seen what happens when this preparation for dying well is neglected.

My own mother left us just about as simply as she came into the world. When she was my age, she sold her home and moved into independent living. When she couldn't manage that any more, we moved her near us into assisted living. When her health failed, she went into a nursing home. At each level of care more and more of her things were given away, until when she finally passed away at ninety-three, I had only to fill a couple of bags with what remained. A Benedictine friend also in her seventies is trying to honor the Rule of Benedict's expectation that monastics are not to own things as individuals but that all is to be held in common for the benefit of the community, as in the book of Acts. All of my friend's belongings are contained in a room the size of my high school bedroom. Recently she went through what she had left and gave away things she had treasured for many years. The message is clear: as we approach the end of life, if we have not already done so, we are to simplify and detach. These are truly spiritual practices. We need very little as we prepare to leave this earthly existence.

Those who have been intentionally walking the spiritual path for many years at some point realize that they are on a journey of transformation that culminates in the life to come. Wherever we have left off on this side of death, we will pick up on the other side. As we age and death approaches, our consciousness shifts and expands. No longer is our focus fixed on the details of daily living, the "getting and spending" through which we lay waste our powers, as the poet Wordsworth observed. The doorway to the divine pathway begins to open and is glimpsed as so inviting that it draws us to it like a magnet. We feel the vibration of its pure loving energy filling our hearts, our souls. We long to fully enter that place where there is no more pain or fear or the limitations of the physical realm, not even of death. The end of our biological life becomes our ultimate freedom, our ticket to a fulfilling new life. As the body fails, the things of earth fade and the things of eternity begin to reveal themselves. Our ultimate mystical experience is to pass through this doorway that is death and re-enter that state of being that is our true home.

For those whose spiritual growth and years of practice have led them to the thin places where the two realms meet and for those who have had life-changing near-death experiences, there is little fear in reaching the moment of death. While we are reluctant to leave behind those we love and the life we have created with them, we know through faith and experience that love is stronger than death and connects us for all eternity.

Following the spiritual path on which we are led, trusting in God's mercy and love, with healed relationships and thoughtful legacies in place, we can live fulfilling lives for as long or as short a time as we are given. Whether we are taken suddenly or die at a ripe old age, we may approach death for what it is: the doorway to eternal life.

EIGHT

The Afterlife

THE SUBJECT OF THE afterlife has been much on my mind of late. Having come face to face with my own death, Alden's, and now Tyler's, it sometimes feels as though the two realms, here and there, are one. Also, my prayer partner and I help some who get stuck in the antechamber of the afterlife continue on their journeys through death, calling on the Communion of Saints for assistance.

Surely all of us have questions about what happens after death. Where do our loved ones go when they leave their bodies behind? Does their consciousness morph into another state of being? How can we stay connected with them when their physical presence is no more? What does the church have to say about the three other last things: judgment, hell, and heaven? How does the Christian tradition's understanding of these compare to that of people who have crossed at least partially through the threshold of death and then have come back to life, those who have had a near-death experience or something like it?

In reflecting on my extraordinary time, I became interested in the church's doctrine of purgatory and the intermediate state to which souls are said to go after death if they die in the faith. As a lifelong Protestant and for nearly twenty years a Presbyterian minister before becoming Catholic, I knew little of purgatory. Martin Luther and certain Reformers of the sixteenth century dismissed the doctrine, believing that God's grace alone led the souls of believers to heaven and eternal life with Christ. I also wanted to explore more fully the tradition's understanding of and experience with the Communion of Saints, that body of all believers through the ages, so researching these areas in depth became a summer's project.

During this time I visited a friend in Oregon, an oblate of a women's Benedictine monastery. She invited a couple of the sisters to lunch at her home while I was there. When one of them asked what I'd been doing lately, I replied that I'd been reading a dozen or more books about purgatory and trying to figure out what to believe about it. This unexpected response led us into a fascinating conversation, one I've been having with a number of sisters, monastics, priests, and those who grew up in the Catholic faith about their understanding of the nature and significance of purgatory.

Why should this be of interest to the general reader at this point? Because purgatory is the Christian explanation for that intermediate state to which many religions believe souls migrate after death. It is not the highest realm—heaven for Christians—but on the way there. Only martyrs and those destined for sainthood go straight to heaven, according to the early church's tradition. Anyone who has made the decision for Christ before death is assured of heaven eventually but not before putting in time being purged of whatever still stands in the way of entering into the full light of the presence of God.

We will return to purgatory in a moment, but before one arrives there, the tradition teaches us that the next of the last things, judgment, takes place. We are given glimpses of the last judgment in the gospels, most especially in the familiar prophetic passage in Matthew 25:31–46 when Jesus returns in his glory and sits on his judgment seat. He then separates all those who failed to serve the poor and suffering from the righteous, who did. The first group, like goats sorted out from the herd of sheep, is dispatched into eternal punishment, while the second, like the sheep of the Good Shepherd, enters into eternal life. Actually, the tradition teaches of two judgments: one takes place immediately upon death, the particular judgment, and the other, the final judgment, like the one described in Matthew, happens at the second coming of Christ when all things are reconciled and gathered to himself. Then, what we have prayed for aeons in the Lord's Prayer will be fulfilled: "Thy will be done on earth as it is in heaven."

What concerns us here is that first judgment, the particular one which happens right after death. According to hundreds of accounts, not only of those who have had NDEs but also in the annals of the Christian tradition, as soon as we pass through death to the next state of being we are taken through an accounting of our lives. All that we have said and done throughout our lives is replayed as though in fast-forward mode in a matter of what would be the equivalent of minutes if time existed in the same way over there, which it doesn't. Time apparently has sequence, that is, before and after, but is not linear as we experience it here. During this accounting, often called the life review, we not only remember and feel every thought and emotion we had throughout our lives, but—and this is the hard part—we experience what those with whom we interacted and may have hurt felt during and after our interactions. And we are able to understand the consequences and ripple effects of our behaviors. To balance these, we also find out the positive effects of our thoughts and actions over our lifetimes.

What could be a more perfect judgment? It's us being shown, as on a movie reel, not only the story of our lives but the impact we had on others. Those who have experienced this life review during their clinical deaths and returned among the living have remarked that it's both very painful and very loving to have a chance to really see the effects we have had while alive. It's a brilliant way of not casting us among the goats but letting us know the impacts of our thoughts, feelings, and actions—good, bad, and ugly. There's great grace and justice in that. What we experience during that time could be compared to some accounts of purgatory, which I'll soon describe. If, after we have been met by our loved ones on the other side, the life review is the first significant thing that happens in the afterlife, it supports what I was saying in the last chapter about the need to heal relationships and make amends for our harmful and thoughtless acts while we are alive, so that our life reviews take into account our changed hearts.

One of the dimensions of this experience NDE survivors commonly describe is the sense that everything and everyone in the universe is interconnected, united in a field of divine love with an actual fabric of filaments that appear like fibers of light. In my healing work years ago I used to refer to the phenomenon of this interwoven fabric of connectivity as the unified field of love of which we are all a part but are largely unaware in our dense world and physical bodies. If everything is connected and moving into ever closer, more loving relationship, it is no wonder that during the life review this sense of oneness allows the newly released soul to feel and see in exquisite detail the impact of his or her life on the web of all life.

This particular judgment, which for the fully or newly conscious is a self-judgment as much as a divine one, is the one that determines where we spend the first part of eternity: hell, that state of being cast out from the presence of Christ because those sent there have chosen it for themselves by their actions and unbelief; heaven, for those exceptional souls like the saints and martyrs who have lived and died with purity of heart; or, for the vast majority of us, that intermediate state called purgatory, where we endure further trials and undergo purging but are assured eventually of heaven. This is the state so many faithful believers have trouble believing in. I did, too, at first. One book I read, written by a Jesuit priest, Fr. Francis X. Schouppe, *Purgatory*, published in 1920, documented hundreds of reliable accounts of saints, priests, religious, and lay people who received communications and visitations from loved ones who had crossed over and were experiencing the pains and pangs of purgatory. These visitors from the other side begged for prayers and Masses to be said for them that they might be released from purgatory into heaven. One of these was the brother of the great Dominican theologian and mystic St. Thomas Aquinas, who is reported to have returned after the saint had successfully prayed him into heaven to thank him for his good offices.

What are we to make of such accounts? This was a question I put to over a dozen priests and sisters of my acquaintance in numerous conversations. Not one of them believed in a purgatory in which people suffered the pains of fire and ice that the older accounts report. Rather, they generally accepted that following death we are still on a spiritual journey to God that is incomplete and that we are not punished but lovingly supported on that journey.

Purgatory is certainly not a physical place, as was long believed in the tradition, located in the geography of the nether regions nearer to hell than heaven. For centuries many of the faithful thought one could enter purgatory through a cave on an island in Lough Derg, County Donegal, Ireland, where legend had it St. Patrick had visions of suffering souls in need of prayer and God's mercy. Thereafter for many centuries pilgrimages were made to "St. Patrick's Purgatory," as it was known. Pilgrims attempted to experience the suffering and deprivations of purgation while still living so as to avoid them after death.[1]

In a somewhat similar way, the *Penitentes* I knew about when I lived in New Mexico, secret brotherhoods in mostly Hispanic rural areas, would imitate the suffering of Christ, especially during Holy Week. They would engage in flagellation, carry heavy crosses for long distances, and be tied or even nailed onto their crosses. They considered these practices penance to expiate their own sinfulness by sharing in Christ's torments. Other cultures encourage the practice of crawling on one's knees to a sacred site to pray for forgiveness, or even more extreme measures. Most of us are familiar

---

1. See Pasula, *Heaven Can Wait*.

with the great, ancient pilgrimage route from Germany or France through Spain, the Camino de Compostela, which ends at the cathedral, Santiago de Compostela, the burial site of St. James. Pilgrimages were usually undertaken as penance during the holy season of Lent in order to share in Christ's suffering.

One conclusion I carry away from my extraordinary time is that there's more than enough suffering in this life without taking our spiritual practices to extremes. A Benedictine abbot I know recently talked about not allowing uncommon measures like lengthy or severe fasting among his monks. Not only is it harmful to their health but it also singles them out from the community as potentially "holier than thou." St. Benedict believed in moderation and meaningful sacrifice, such as in the choice of one's vocation or living arrangements, not punishing the body for its human passions.

These kinds of beliefs and practices concerning purgatory were not those of the deeply formed religious to whom I spoke. Not one of them believed that a loving and merciful God would require this degree of suffering as expiation for sin. Nearly all envision purgatory as a state of being in which we are assured of God's grace and are helped to learn what we still need to know and to experience unconditional love before we are ready for the full light of God's presence. That is the understanding of purgatory or the intermediate state which makes sense to me. It's another way of saying, as Jesus did to his disciples, that in the realms of God, there are many dwelling places.[2] Not all of us go immediately to the same place, or state of being, because we didn't end life in the same state of being. Some leave angry or depressed or haven't yet awakened into a higher consciousness. Others of the faithful are still near the beginning of their deeper spiritual journeys. The help these souls receive and what they experience at first will be different from that of those who are further along on their spiritual paths. And those at the higher levels or broader plains in the realms of light teach and support those who aren't yet ready to move further on.

From the accounts I've read and heard, the intermediate state almost seems like a school where those at similar levels are divided into classes and encouraged to advance through the grades by wise, devoted teachers. We are encouraged to explore and experience all the beauty and marvels that open before us. If we haven't fully learned our spiritual lessons, we are given another chance, good instruction, and support to more fully develop our

2. John 14:2.

understanding of God, God's love, and the cosmic realms where everything is connected through that love. And all of this happens within a supportive community, part of the larger Communion of Saints.

Seen in this way, purgatory, or that process through which our hearts and souls are purified by the love of God within the body of Christ, doesn't seem punitive at all, but merciful and gracious. We are the recipients first of God's justice during the life review, then of God's mercy as we are forgiven our errors and patterns of sinfulness revealed during the review. Afterwards, we are encouraged to learn what we didn't understand about God and God's creation when we were alive and are able to experience God's unconditional love in community.

This view of purgatory also obviates the apparent need of so many contemporary spiritual seekers to believe in past lives, karma, and reincarnation, borrowed from other ancient faith traditions but not a part of the Christian understanding. Our "ascension" toward the higher realms of light happens over there, not here on earth again, as though we needed to come back and repeat our errors time after time until we get things right. Where's the love in that? If we believe that our actions have karmic consequences, our idea of justice may be to go through many lifetimes until we have balanced our karmic debt and reached enlightenment. But that's not consistent with the grace of God we find in the Christian tradition.

A recent morning prayer excerpt from Psalm 103 confirmed for me the grace-filled pattern of justice, mercy, and love: "The Lord is merciful and gracious, slow to anger and abounding in steadfast love. He will not always accuse, nor will he keep his anger forever. He does not deal with us according to our sins, nor repay us according to our iniquities. For as the heavens are high above the earth, so great is his steadfast love toward those who fear him."[3]

The more we are able to understand and accept with humility and gratitude God's justice and mercy in this life, the more we will live out that refining process which is purgatory here and now, not just in the hereafter on our journey toward union with God within the unified field of love. That understanding of the living experience of purgatory is what, finally, lights up my own extraordinary time and makes it add up to so much more than an inexplicable random experience of intense suffering, death, and transition. It was, quite literally, a time of exquisite enlightenment.

---

3. Ps 103:8–11.

My recent musings on these last things were greatly illumined by theologian Joseph Ratzinger (later Pope Benedict XVI) in his scholarly and pastoral work first published in 1977, *Eschatology: Death and Eternal Life.* I was not expecting to be so taken by Cardinal Ratzinger's book, as my Benedictine friends consider him one of the more conservative popes in recent times, but I found this book brilliant and surprisingly accessible. "The essential Christian understanding of Purgatory is the inwardly necessary process of transformation in which a person becomes capable of Christ, capable of God and thus capable of unity with the whole communion of saints," he wrote. "It does not replace grace by works, but allows the former to achieve its full victory precisely as grace. What actually saves is the full assent of faith . . . . The root of the Christian doctrine of Purgatory is the christological grace of penance. Purgatory follows by an inner necessity from the idea of penance, the idea of the constant readiness for reform which marks the forgiven sinner."[4]

As my Protestant friends would say, grace is given first so that we can accept our brokenness and experience the contrition leading to penance. Ratzinger states that "The Reformation called Purgatory into question in face of deformed practices,"[5] probably like the ones described in the historic and cultural accounts above, rather than because it was an inherently flawed doctrine. Accepting our intermediate state acknowledges that we have a distance to go on what I have called the path of the purified heart before we are ready to stand before the throne of God and join the choirs of angels in endless praise to God's glory. And that leads us to why we pray for the dead and why they pray for us.

Recently, on the second Sunday of Advent in Year B of the three-year lectionary cycle of scriptural readings, the New Testament selection was from Second Peter. I first really engaged this text in seminary when assigned to preach on it at chapel for the whole community. Hearing it as though for the first time, it absolutely stunned me. What I understood then through faith and now also through experience is that God is waiting for us to be ready before the days of the final reconciliation between heaven and earth takes place. Listen:

> The Lord is not slow about his promise, as some think of slowness, but is patient with you, not wanting any to perish, but all to come to repentance. But the day of the Lord will come like a thief,

4. Ratzinger, *Eschatology,* 230–33.

5. Ibid., 219.

and then the heavens will pass away with a loud noise, and the
elements will be dissolved with fire, and the earth and everything
that is done on it will be disclosed. Since all these things are to be
dissolved in this way what sort of person ought you to be in leading lives of holiness and godliness, waiting for and hastening the
coming of the day of God, because of which the heavens will be set
ablaze and dissolved, and the elements will melt with fire? But in
accordance with his promise, we wait for new heavens and a new
earth, where righteousness is at home.[6]

This passage, one on which I have reflected in sustained *Lectio Divina*
for many years, reveals the incredibly all-encompassing graciousness of our
God, who waits patiently to include even the most recalcitrant among the
body of Christ, the Communion of Saints, so that the final consummation
of human life may be fulfilled through its integration into and full union
with God. That ultimately is the end of our spiritual journeys, when all of
earth is heaven with all souls who have ever lived joined in one community,
one body. That is what we pray for when we pray, "Come, Lord Jesus." We
wait, then, not just for God to make up God's mind to send Jesus back for
the second coming, the final judgment, but for ourselves to be ready for it!
Our own spiritual growth contributes to that of the whole body because
of our interconnectedness and hastens the day of the Lord. It's not going
to come unless and until we contribute to bringing it about. So we as the
people of God have a responsibility to pray for those not only here on earth
to move along on their spiritual paths but also those in the intermediate
state to reach full union with God. And those who are on their way are also
prayed for by the saints who have gotten there ahead of the rest of us.

Cardinal Ratzinger says this about the nature of heaven: "If heaven
depends on being in Christ, then it must involve a co-being with all those
who, together, constitute the body of Christ . . . . It is the open society
of the Communion of Saints and in this way the fulfillment of human
communion."[7] In a lovely image he goes on to say that "The Communion
of Saints represents the unruptured self-communion of the whole body
of Christ and the closeness of a love which knows no limit and is sure of
attaining God in the neighbor and the neighbor in God."[8] Later he confirms
that heaven will only be complete "when all the members of the Lord's

6. 2 Pet 3: 9–13.
7. Ratzinger, *Eschatology*, 235.
8. Ibid., 237.

body are gathered in." That's when the resurrection of the body will take place, the *parousia,* and the presence of Christ "will reach its fullest and encompass all those who are to be saved and the whole cosmos with them." In this way, heaven comes in two stages: "The individual's salvation is whole and entire only when the salvation of the cosmos and all the elect has come to full fruition. For the redeemed are not simply adjacent to each other in heaven. Rather, in their being together as the one Christ, they are heaven. In that moment, the whole creation will become song. It will be a single act in which, forgetful of self, the individual will break through the limits of being into the whole, and the whole takes up its dwelling in the individual. It will be joy in which all questioning is resolved and satisfied."[9] To this I say, *Amen! Alleluia!* I find it an inspirational explanation of God's intentions for God's people and the whole of creation, of why the *parousia* is worth waiting for, and of what we are to do in the meantime to help bring about that joyous moment when the whole creation will become song.

From this highest of highs, we drop for a moment to the lowest of lows: what, you may ask, about hell? Aren't there some, like Satan and his minions, just too far gone to be brought into that oneness of the Communion of Saints within the unified field of love? What about Hitler and serial killers? I respond with another question. What was Jesus doing on the day before his resurrection in his spirit body? The Nicene Creed asserts that he descended into hell. The Harrowing of Hell, as this action by Christ is known, is not scriptural but is a strong part of the tradition. On the wall next to my desk is an icon of the Harrowing of Hell. Icons are possibly the most sacred form of art, that is, the closest to their source rather than open to individual interpretation, like most later art. While written by different icon-writers, the composition and symbolism of each is the same. Icons revealed to early Christians who had no access to written texts the substance and levels of meaning of the most important Scriptures. In this classic icon, the risen Christ, dressed in a snowy white robe, stands on a pure white broken cross, signifying his victory over death. There in hell, according to the tradition, he freed those souls born before his coming, including the great prophets of Israel, like Moses, on his right hand, and, on his left, those chief culprits of human sin, Adam and Eve. He is shown reaching down from his position on his broken cross to raise them up. Archangels situated above Christ oversee and witness this act of mercy and

9. Ibid., 238.

grace on the part of the Crucified One whose resurrection from the dead foreshadows the full bodily resurrection promised at his second coming.

Like purgatory, hell is a state of being, in this case one of separation from God through ignorance or willful choice—or both, I would say. Will not Christ make every effort to rescue even those who have refused him again and again? Isn't their redemption part of what we await and which our prayers for them would aid? I'm not speaking of people of other faiths and those who have lived moral lives, but rather of those who have given in to the dark side, who have committed such evil acts that their souls are darkened. And yet even in hell, contrary to Dante's *Inferno*, there is hope. The beautiful prologue to John's gospel confirms that "the light shines in the darkness, and the darkness did not overcome it."[10] The darkness cannot overcome the light, but the light can and will overcome the darkness.

As Cardinal Ratzinger observed, while we must hold onto "God's unconditional respect for the freedom of his creature" who can be transformed through love, "the damned have the right to will their own damnation."[11] And yet Jesus descended into hell. Ratzinger comments that for saints like Therese de Lisieux and John of the Cross hell isn't so much a threat to others as a challenge to oneself "to suffer in the dark night of faith, to experience communion with Christ in solidarity with his descent into the Night. One draws near to the Lord's radiance by sharing his darkness. One serves the salvation of the world by leaving one's own salvation behind for the sake of others."[12] This elevates suffering with and for others to new heights, as the saints through the ages have modeled for us. Ratzinger goes on to say that "The doctrine of everlasting punishment preserves its real content. The idea of mercy, which has accompanied it, in one form or another, throughout its long history, must not become a theory. Rather is it the prayer of suffering, hopeful faith."[13] So we as the body of Christ on earth and in heaven pray also for those who have consigned themselves to hell as well as those who have not yet found heaven. We seek to enter with Christ into their darkness and show them how to find his light. When hell empties out because no one is left there, we will know the end times are near.

We turn once more to the subject of the Communion of Saints because this communion is what shall become our ultimate identity. Throughout

10. John 1:5.

11. Ratzinger, *Eschatology,* 216.

12. Ibid., 217–18.

13. Ibid., 218.

this book I have spoken about "my" Communion of Saints, those whom I have identified as loving their neighbor—in this case, me—as themselves, whether they are of the Christian faith or not. Those women and men, children, and, yes, animal companions, who show selfless love reflecting God's unconditional love for us are well on their way to an afterlife of joy and peace. Since the many faith communions within Christianity have differing understandings of what constitutes the Communion of Saints, I will hold to the simple definition that it is the full body of Christ among both the living and the dead, as well as the angelic realm.

One of my favorite pieces of liturgical music is the Litany of the Saints, sung at Mass at the Easter Vigil and on feast days of the martyrs. It begins with the *Kyrie*, "Lord, have mercy," then moves to name the great saints of the church, asking them to pray for us: "Mary and Joseph, Michael and all angels," chants the cantor. The people respond, "Pray for us." This pattern then moves through the saints of the Old Testament, the New Testament, and the saints and martyrs of the church's long tradition. Some versions include the favorite saints of the community which is singing the litany. It ends with a prayer to the Lord Jesus to hear his people and to show them his mercy and salvation. This moving invocation of the Communion of Saints led by Christ illustrates beautifully what the body of Christ is about and how we may access the saints who have gone before us during our lifetimes.

One of the treasured aspects of the devotional lives of Catholics I have come to appreciate is praying through—not to—the saints. We ask those special saints who are associated with particular causes or whom we have come to know and love to pray for us or those for whom we are concerned. I have a constellation of my own favorites now. They include Mother Mary, the subject of so much Catholic devotion; Mary Magdalene; Benedict, of course, and his twin sister, Scholastica; Columba, Hildegard of Bingen, Dominic, Francis, Thomas Aquinas, Paul, Ignatius of Loyola, Teresa of Avila, John of the Cross; Elizabeth Ann Seton, whose relic was gifted to me during my illness; the great healer, Pio (Padre Pio); another healer on his way to sainthood, Blessed Solanus Casey, a Capuchin brother; and the Carmelite Edith Stein (Theresa Benedicta of the Cross). I include a couple of others not yet recognized as saints but candidates for whom I would advocate: Julian of Norwich and the Venerable Maria de Agreda, a seventeenth-century Franciscan mystic with whom Mother Mary shared her life story, as recorded in the monumental *The Mystical City of God*. I love many of the other mystics and healers as well and often invoke them in prayer. I have found that if you call upon them they may indeed hear you and respond, even if you aren't aware of their presence or prayers on your behalf. It gives us a company of advanced souls to intercede for us and our loved ones and to learn from about how to live a sustained holy life. They support us on our spiritual paths, always encouraging and sometimes consoling.

Occasionally I read biographies of those saints to whom I am drawn and invite them to read along with me and reveal themselves to me in whatever ways they will. This has been very enlightening. Just as we may carry on a colloquy with Jesus, we may converse with one of the saints or angelic presences, even though it may at times seem like a one-way conversation. By inviting a two-way communication, we are developing loving relationships with those we will someday meet face to face. My own beloved husband, Alden, is now among the Communion of Saints in the intermediate state, and I experience his presence from time to time. Even my sweet Tyler is not far away. In fact, we may occupy the same physical space, just in different dimensions. Since heaven and purgatory are states of being rather than places, it's a matter of our vibrational energy pairing up when the conditions are right so that we can sense or even see or hear each other's presence.

The point toward which we have been moving is that the dead are not dead but alive in another way and, although it is more difficult to connect with them then before, they have not entirely disappeared. As we know, love is stronger than death, and we will in all likelihood be greeted by them when our time comes to cross through death. I love the image in Isaiah 35 of the highway in the desert called the Holy Way: "the redeemed of the Lord shall walk there and the ransomed of the Lord shall return, and come to Zion with singing; everlasting joy shall be upon their heads; they shall obtain joy and gladness, and sorrow and sighing shall flee away."[14] It brings to mind the Communion of Saints marching into heaven, as in the old spiritual, "When the Saints Go Marching In," and the great cloud of witnesses, the martyrs and saints, by which we are surrounded, according to Hebrews.[15] When our own sojourns through the intermediate state are over, we will join these ranks and move into the higher, even more glorious realms of light.

14. Isa 35:9–10.
15. Heb 12:1.

These teachings of the church and its tradition sustained me through my extraordinary time and continue to provide great comfort and hope. So have the accounts of those who have had an NDE or other spiritually transformative experience. Although they may not know how to interpret them, these encounters with the afterlife truly transform those who have had them and set them on intentional spiritual paths. I encourage those serious seekers to find wise, reliable guides among the church's Communion of Saints.

I personally have known quite a few people who have had NDEs or NDE-like experiences. I'm sure most of you do too, even though they may not have shared these with you. They are not easy to talk about but are unforgettable, and those who have them are likely to use them for sustained *Lectio Divina* throughout their lives, as did Julian of Norwich. A close friend only told me of her NDE a few months ago when I raised the subject. We have neither the language nor the conceptual framework for communicating to others what went on during the experience, which usually lasts only a few minutes, and how it has changed us. Also, the experiences may feel too precious and mysterious to share, especially if we fear being judged by others who don't know what to make of them as imagining or making up our stories.

For many years NDEs were challenged by scientists and medical doctors as not credible. However, much research has been conducted since Dr. Raymond A. Moody, Jr.'s groundbreaking book, *Life After Life*, was first published in 1975, and many credible people have come forward to share their own NDEs. Moody and others founded the International Association for Near-Death Studies (IANDS) in 1978 as a vehicle for research on NDEs and NDE-like experiences, and the organization now is active globally and in nearly every state in the US. When Dr. Eben Alexander, a neurosurgeon, published the account of his extended NDE in 2012 in *Proof of Heaven,* and orthopedic surgeon Mary C. Neal's *To Heaven and Back* appeared the same year, popular acceptance of NDEs dramatically increased. Both of these scientifically trained physicians tried to account for their extraordinary experiences through logic but finally had to accept another kind of truth that comes from knowing through experience. Interestingly, both Alexander and Neal have published subsequent, fuller accounts of their NDEs and their personal transformations after reflecting on their experiences for several years. Nearly every day you can find another published account of someone's near-death experience and how it transformed his or her life.

In *Life After Life* Moody identified fifteen markers common to NDEs, such as the familiar out-of-body experience of floating above one's dead body and observing what was going on around it, passage through a dark tunnel toward a bright light, being met by loving beings, reaching a barrier, and either being told to go back into the body or given a choice to do so. Some stay on the other side long enough to experience the life review mentioned earlier. Moody's more recent book, *Reflections on Life After Life* (2011), includes other markers common in the thousands of cases he has encountered. Dr. Kenneth Ring's *Lessons from the Light* (2006) has also become something of a classic in the field of NDEs. In addition, transformative experiences similar to or related to NDEs have been identified and researched in recent years, including near-death-like Experiences, shared near-death experiences, and even spiritually transformative experiences, all of which really are glimpses into and encounters with the great beyond that change our understanding of reality and bring about substantive shifts in our consciousness and often lead to dramatic life changes. I have had several of these kinds of experiences myself, as has my son, and they have been common to mystics and contemplatives of all faiths through the ages. What this adds up to is a growing acknowledgement that human consciousness does not end at death but survives and passes into another dimension, from which it may further evolve until it reaches an enlightened union with the divine, the state Christians know as heaven.

What, then, might we learn from these accounts that can help us during our remaining lives on earth? That is a question which Fr. Matt Linn, SJ, and his partners, Dennis and Sheila Linn, answered in their intriguing book mentioned earlier, *The Gifts of Near-Death Experiences: You Don't Have to Die to Experience Your True Home* (2016). Using some of Dr. Moody's NDE markers and drawing from the work of Dr. Kenneth Ring, who became a friend, the Linns explore in particular depth the experiences of meeting loved ones in the realms of light and the life review, leading to suggested exercises for healing ourselves, our false perceptions, and our damaged relationships through the power of unconditional love. I commend this book to you, along with the online video seminar the Linns provide on this subject at www.linnministries.org.

In the same way that Drs. Alexander and Neal offer a bridge between science and spirituality through the accounts of their NDEs, the Linns offer a groundbreaking bridge between the Christian faith tradition in which they are firmly rooted and the growing body of spiritual seekers exploring sources of wisdom and enlightenment on their own. These glimpses into the afterlife from both scientists and religious leaders are helping to bring about a new synthesis of science and spirituality, surely the work of the Holy Spirit!

Too many of us have felt we had to reach outside the borders of our traditional religion and faith communions to find the love, wisdom, and community we desire. I hope I have at least partially succeeded in showing that these three gifts have always been at the heart of the Christian faith and tradition. They are what guided me back into the church years ago after I had left for a time of personal exploration and have grounded and sustained me through these recent most trying times. There is endless depth and spiritual guidance to be found within the framework of the Christian church, and in recent years I have come to see my work as helping spiritual seekers find the points of connection between their urgent hunger for the divine and deep Christian spirituality as it has been practiced over the centuries. To that end, following the publication of my 2012 book, *Path of the Purified Heart: The Spiritual Journey as Transformation,* I was guided by the Holy Spirit to form what became Friends of Christ School for Christian Spirituality, based in Chapel Hill, North Carolina, where I was living at the time. Friends of Christ School (www.friendsofChristschool.com) is an ecumenical gathering place for those who want to deepen their understanding of Christian spirituality and its practices. Participants complete foundational classes, taught by local clergy and experienced teachers, in which they are companioned in small groups by trained spiritual directors who support their spiritual growth. Now in its sixth year, Friends of Christ School has grown into a community bonded by the common pursuit of the things of God and desire for companions on the spiritual journey. It is supported by local congregations that recognize how the School supplements what they are able to offer and assist the School's mission by publicizing and hosting classes and in other ways. The Friends of Christ model was intended to be replicated in other communities where the fresh winds of the Holy Spirit gather core groups of seekers who wish to ground themselves in a tradition in which they can grow and find spiritual guidance and support. I am deeply grateful for the Spirit's guidance and the wonderful spiritual companions I met and worked with through those years with the school and pray that other seekers may find such Spirit-led opportunities in their own communities.

In the end, the afterlife is just that: after life. We may catch an occasional glimpse into its nature and can learn from the experiences and insights of those who have ventured past its threshold and returned. Our faith communions offer guidance in how to prepare for it. But we are still among the land of the living, spiritual beings in human form. What these afterlife studies best encourage, it seems to me, is leading a life filled with love, generosity, faith, hope, and joy so that when we are greeted at those legendary pearly gates we might hear the treasured words of our Master, "Well done, thou good and faithful servant."

As my own date with death and journey to the afterlife approaches, I return occasionally to the words of St. Paul with which I began Part 2 of this book: "For to me, living is Christ and dying is gain. If I am to live in the flesh, that means fruitful labor for me; I do not know which I prefer. I am hard pressed between the two: my desire is to depart and be with Christ, for that is far better; but to remain in the flesh is more necessary for you."[16] Death is a great mystery enveloped within the love of God. It leads to an even greater mystery to be revealed in due time of a shared eternal life with God and the Communion of Saints. I am grateful to have been given the opportunity and capacity to share the story of my extraordinary time, to have survived it all, and to have borne its fruit in these reflections. May they help strengthen you through your own extraordinary times and illumine your passage through the final mystery into the fullness of eternal life!

16. Phil 1:21–24.

Bibliography

Augustine of Hippo. "To Proba," edited by Kevin Knight. http://www.newadvent.org/fathers/1102130.htm.

Church, Dawson. *EFT (Emotional Freedom Techniques) for PTSD (Post Traumatic Stress Disorder)*. Fulton, CA: Energy Psychology, 2017.

DeLorenzo, Leonard J. *Work of Love: A Theological Reconstruction of the Communion of Saints*. Notre Dame, IN: University of Notre Dame Press, 2017.

Dossey, Larry. *Healing Words: The Power of Prayer and the Practice of Medicine*. San Francisco: HarperSanFrancisco, 1994.

———. *One Mind: How Our Individual Mind is Part of a Greater Consciousness . . . And Why It Matters*. Carlsbad, CA: Hay House, 2013.

———. *Prayer is Good Medicine: How to Reap the Healing Benefits of Prayer*. San Francisco: HarperSanFrancisco, 1997.

Dunham, Laura. *Path of the Purified Heart: The Spiritual Journey as Transformation*. Eugene, OR: Cascade, 2012.

Harter, Michael, ed. *Hearts on Fire: Praying with Jesuits*. St. Louis: Jesuit Sources, 1993.

Ignatius of Loyola. *Spiritual Exercises and Selected Works*. Edited by George E. Ganss. New York: Paulist, 1991.

Julian of Norwich. *Showings*. Translated by Edmund Colledge and James Walsh. New York: Paulist, 1978.

Kline, Francis. *Four Ways of Holiness for the Universal Church Drawn from the Monastic Tradition*. Kalamazoo, MI: Cistercian, 2007.

Lewis, C. S. *A Grief Observed*. San Francisco: HarperSanFrancisco, 1994.

Linn, Dennis, Sheila Fabricant Linn, and Matthew Linn. *The Gifts of Near-Death Experiences: You Don't Have to Die to Experience Your True Home*. Charlottesville, VA: Hampton Roads, 2016.

———. *Healing the Future: Personal Recovery from Societal Wounding*. Mahwah, NJ: Paulist, 2012.

———. *Healing the Greatest Hurt*. New York: Paulist, 1985.

MacNutt, Francis. *Healing*. Notre Dame, IN: Ave Maria, 1999.

———. *The Healing Reawakening: Reclaiming Our Lost Inheritance*. Grand Rapids: Chosen, 2005.

Maté, Gabor. *When the Body Says No: Exploring the Stress-Disease Connection*. Hoboken, NJ: John Wiley, 2003.

Moody, Raymond A., Jr. *Life After Life*. New York: HarperOne, 2015.

———. *Reflections on Life After Life.* New York: Bantam/Mockingbird, 2011.

Neal, Mary C. *7 Lessons from Heaven: How Dying Taught Me to Live a Joy-Filled Life.* New York: Convergent, 2017.

O'Connor, Flannery. *The Habit of Being.* Edited by Sally Fitzgerald. New York: Noonday, 1979.

———. *Spiritual Writings.* Edited by Robert Ellsberg. Maryknoll: Orbis, 2003.

Pasula, Diana Walsh. *Heaven Can Wait: Purgatory in Catholic Devotional and Popular Culture.* Oxford: Oxford University Press, 2015.

Rahner, Karl. "Prolixitas Mortis." In "Christian Dying," 226–56. *Theological Investigations* 18. New York: Crossroad, 1976.

Ratzinger, Joseph. *Eschatology: Death and Eternal Life.* 2nd ed. Translated by Michael Waldstein. Washington, DC: The Catholic University of America Press, 1988.

Ring, Kenneth, and Evelyn Elsaesser Valarino. *Lessons from the Light.* Needham, MA: Moment Point, 2000.

Schouppe, Francis X. *Purgatory: Explained by the Lives and Legends of the Saints.* Rockford, IL: TAN, 1986.

Therese of Lisieux. *The Story of a Soul.* Translated and edited by Robert J. Edmonson. Brewster, MA: Paraclete, 2006.

Thiselton, Anthony C. *Life After Death: A New Approach to the Last Things.* Grand Rapids: Eerdmans, 2012.

Walford, Stephen. *Communion of Saints: The Unity of Divine Love in the Mystical Body of Christ.* Kettering, OH: Angelico, 2016.

Wright, Tom. *Surprised by Hope.* London: Society for Promoting Christian Knowledge, 2007.

About the Author

Laura Dunham is a retired Presbyterian minister, now Catholic, and a Benedictine oblate.

She holds a BA in social sciences and an MA and PhD in English. Following careers in higher education and financial planning, she felt God's call to ministry and attended Columbia Theological Seminary. She received an MDiv and later a Certificate in Spiritual Formation from Columbia.

Before retiring, Laura served as a pastor of churches and a governing body and held leadership positions on nonprofit boards of directors. Her 2002 book, *Graceful Living: Your Faith, Values, and Money in Changing Times*, was commissioned by the Ecumenical Stewardship Center. In 2012 Laura published *Path of the Purified Heart: The Spiritual Journey as Transformation* (Cascade Books).

Since her retirement, Laura has engaged in teaching, leading retreats, and writing about Christian spirituality and spiritual formation. In 2012 she led the formation of Friends of Christ School for Christian Spirituality in Chapel Hill, North Carolina. She continues to serve as a consultant and advisor to the school. She is also a Studium Scholar and oblate affiliated with St. Benedict's Monastery in St. Joseph, Minnesota.

Widowed in 2015, Laura now lives in Riverside, California with her son, Tom, and their companion animals. She invites inquiries about her work and visits to her website, www.laura-dunham.com.

CPSIA information can be obtained
at www.ICGtesting.com
Printed in the USA
LVHW111731060219
606612LV00001B/189/P